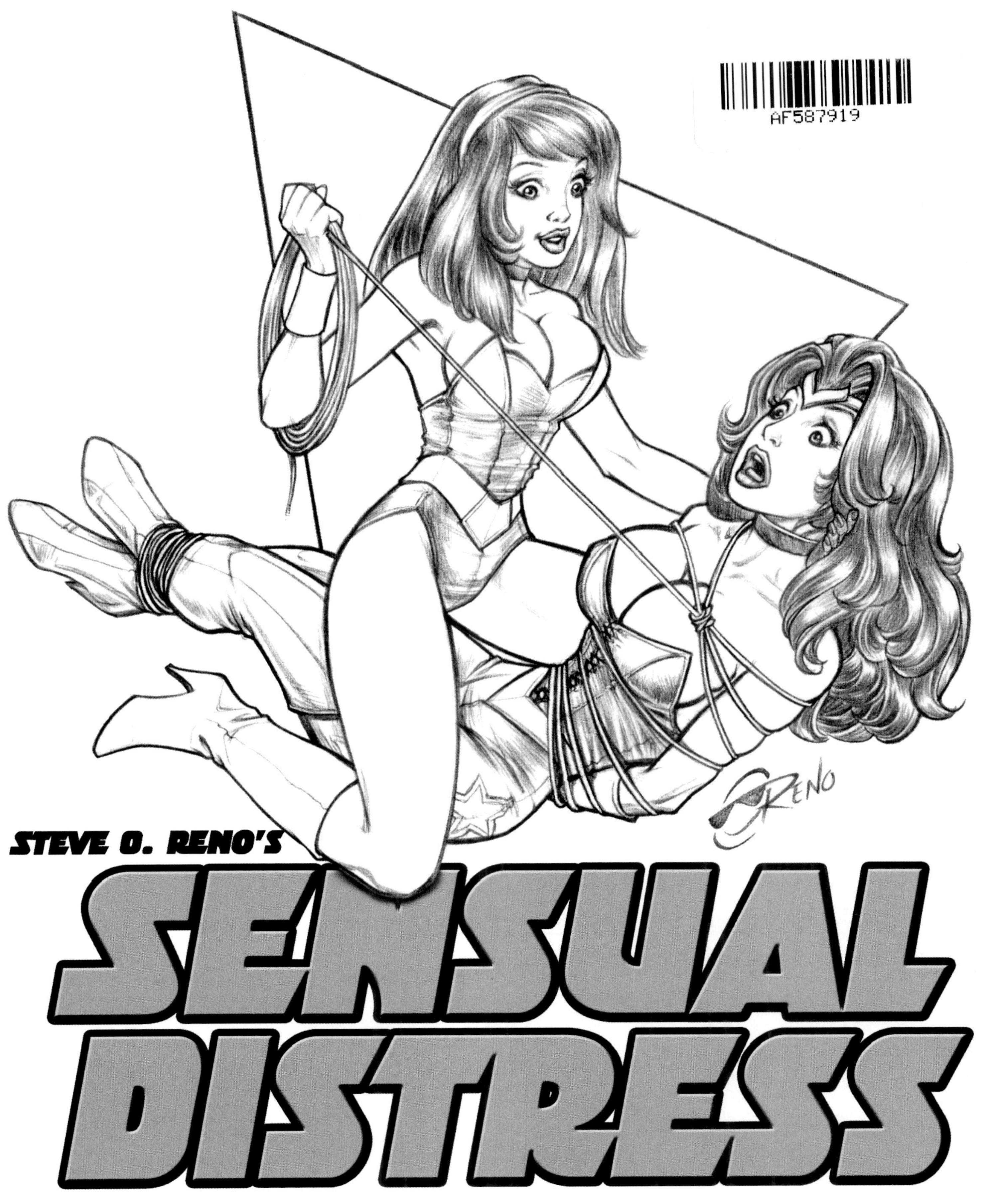

STEVE O. RENO'S

SENSUAL DISTRESS

AN SQP PRESENTATION

What is Sensual Distress?

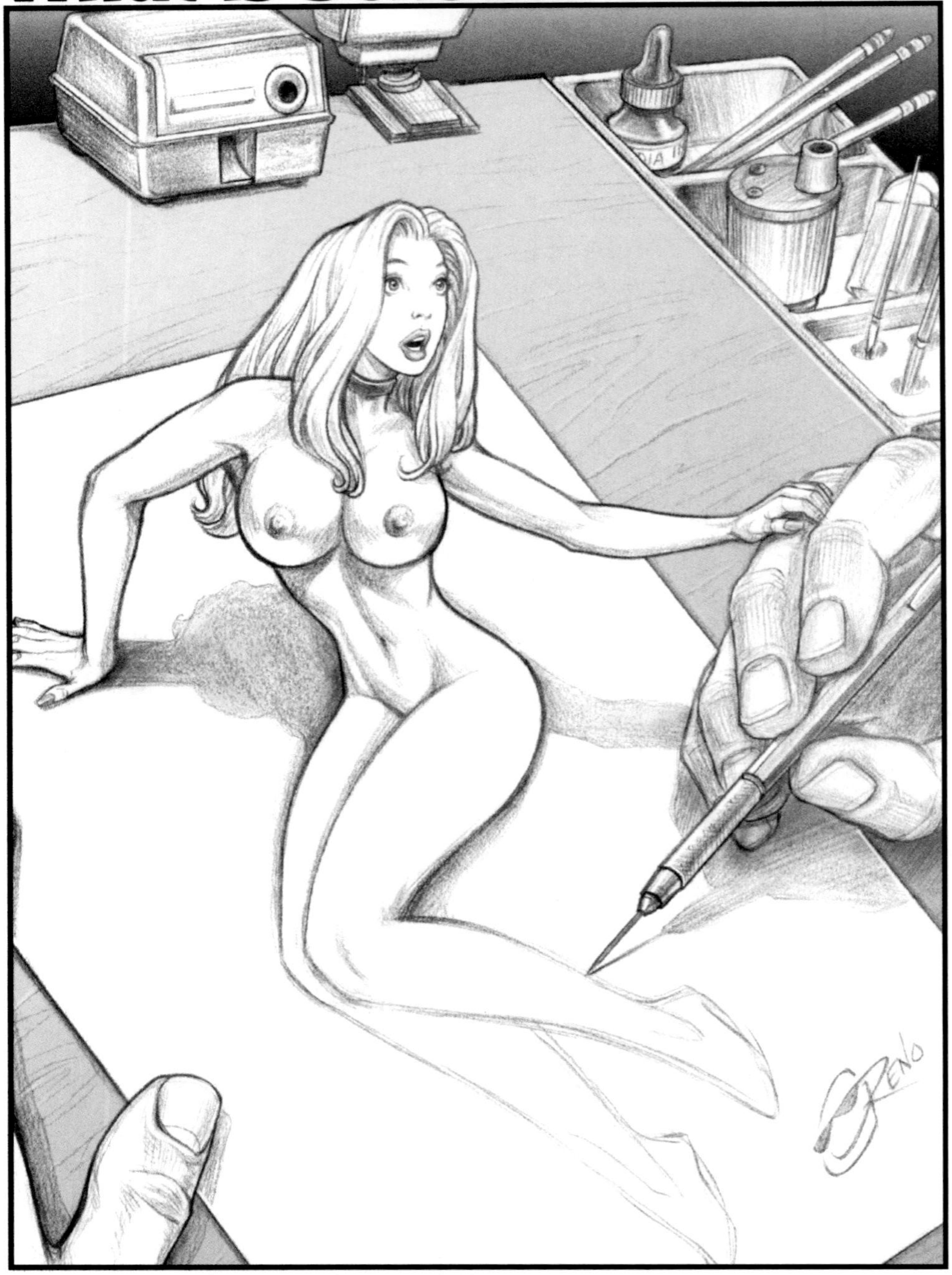

First and foremost it is fantasy. It is sensuality mixed with vulnerability. It is the sexy side of the "Damsel in Distress". It is, simply put, beautiful women in erotic peril. Whether they are bound and gagged, held at the whims of a dastardly villain, or attacked by mysterious creatures with a taste for pleasure, these helpless heroines dance with danger to the delight of the attentive viewer. For some, they make us dream of being a gallant knight who rides in on a fiery steed to rescue the fair princess. For others, they seduce our darker side, making us envious of the villains power over the captured maiden. Then there are those who put themselves in the place of the alluring captive, curious about the variety of sensations she is feeling as her body is provocatively and fiendishly manipulated during her precarious plight, empathizing with the hopelessness of her situation.

It's been said that danger is the greatest thrill, that sex is the deepest desire, and power is the ultimate aphrodisiac. Sensual Distress is a fusion of the three. It can be seen as exciting. It can be seen as perverse. It can arouse and it can incense. It can be a call to the hero inside of us or a temptation to the villain we mask. Within these opposing forces we can find ourselves at times living in both the light and the darkness of our psyche simultaneously. We feel that we would fight the armies of hell to save the helpless heroine, only to find defeat by our own sexual demons. To save the beauty or seize the moment. To rescue or to ravish. To free her or to f... well, you get the idea.

That is the dichotomy of Sensual Distress. To feed the pride of the hero and the greed for his "rewards". To have anger for the villain's deeds but envy for their power. To be gluttonous in our indulgence with all of our lustful instincts and not have to lift a finger... except to turn the page. It's simply sinful!

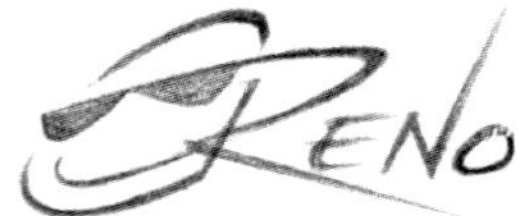

No damsels were harmed in the making of this book.

You can contact Steve O. Reno at
renoart@hotmail.com

Front cover coloring by Mark McNabb

Steve O. Reno's
SENSUAL DISTRESS
Volume One

Book design by Grassy Knoll Studios.
Publishers: Sal Quartuccio and Bob Keenan
Published by
SQP Inc.
PO Box 248 - Columbus, NJ 08022

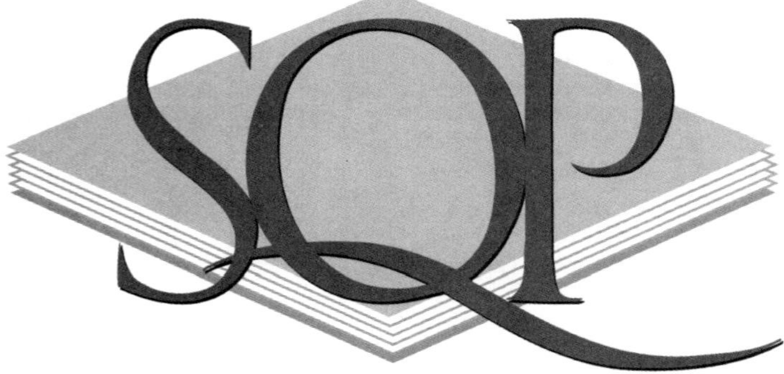

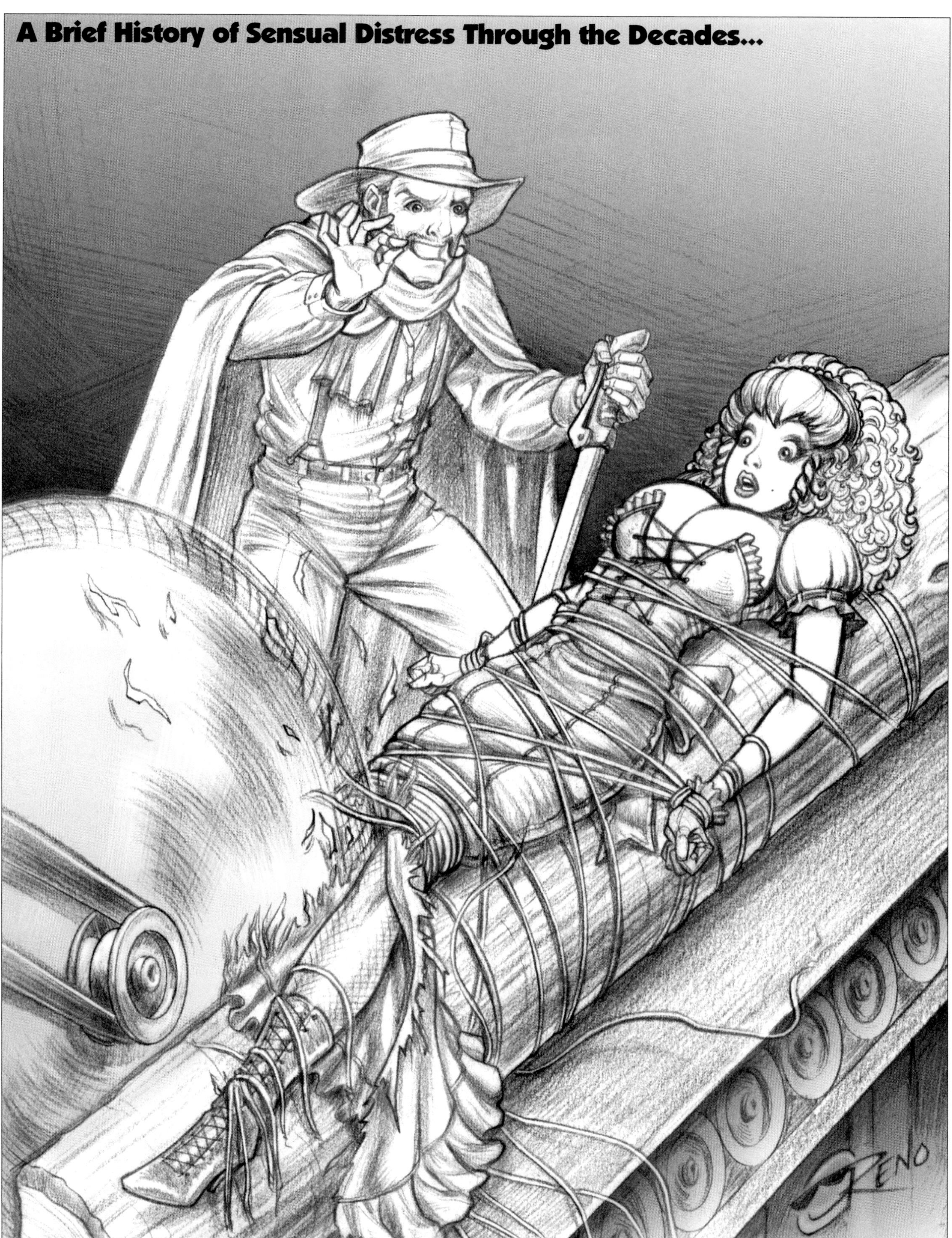

1920's - The Buzzsaw

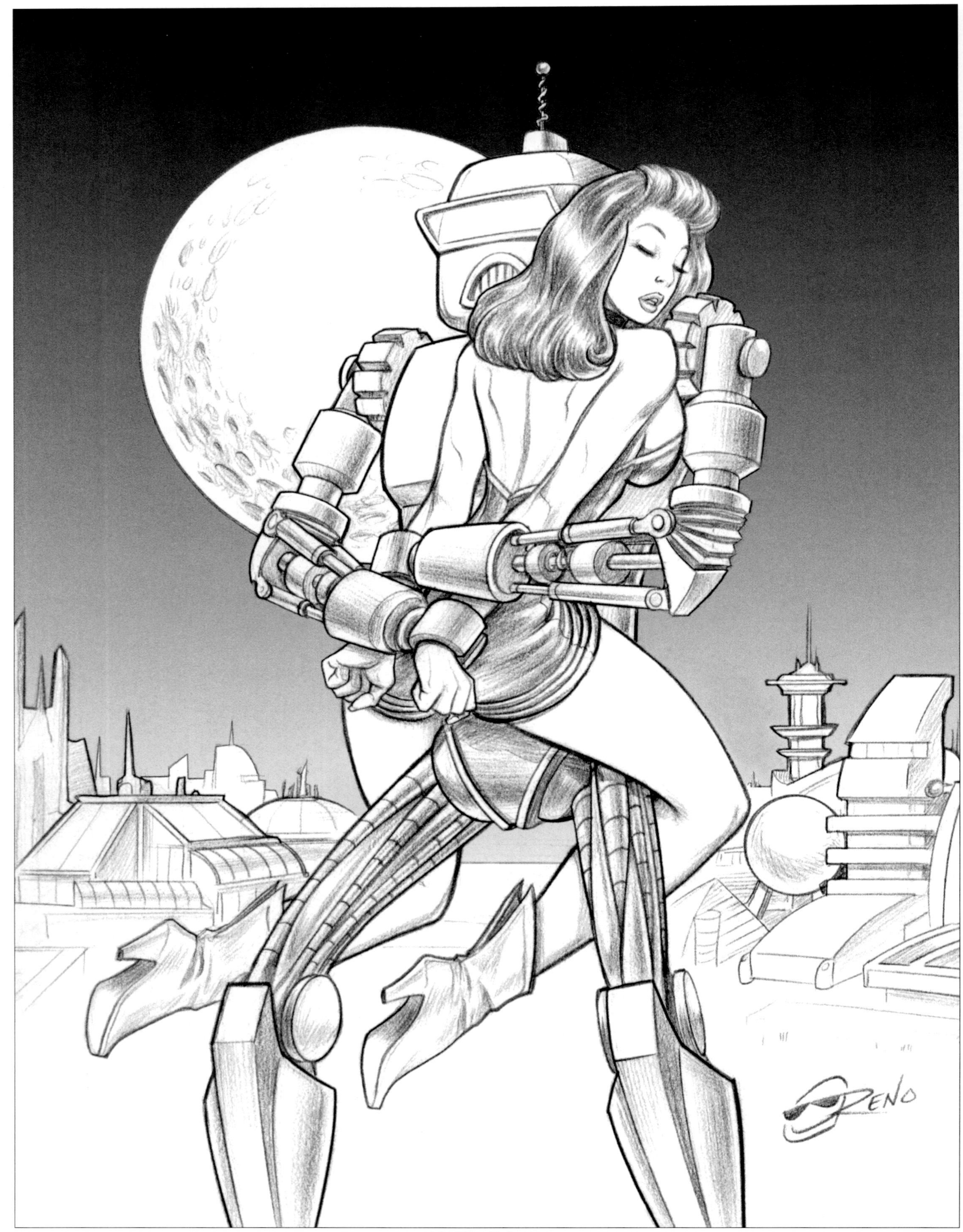

1930's - Robotica

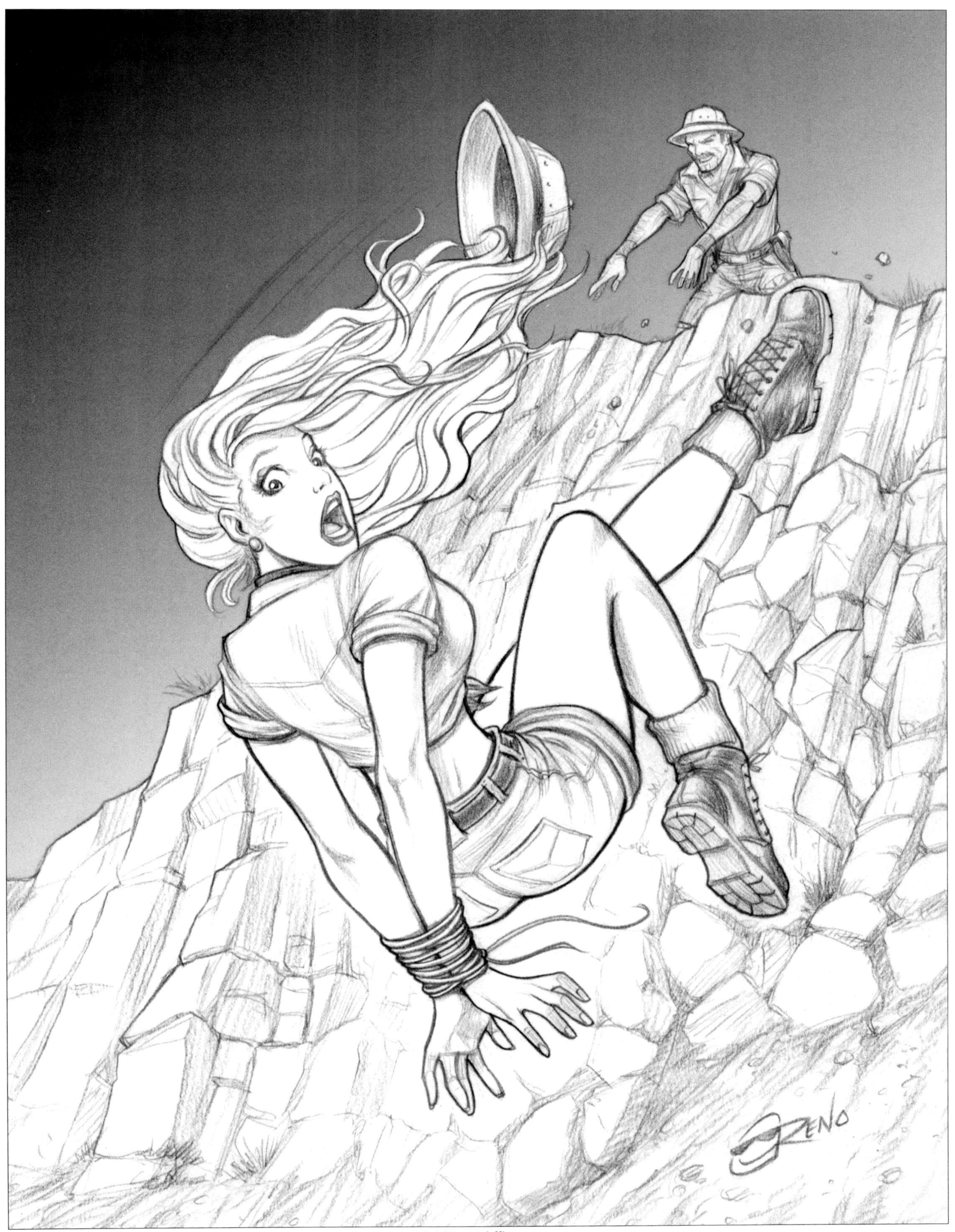

1940's - Cliffhanger

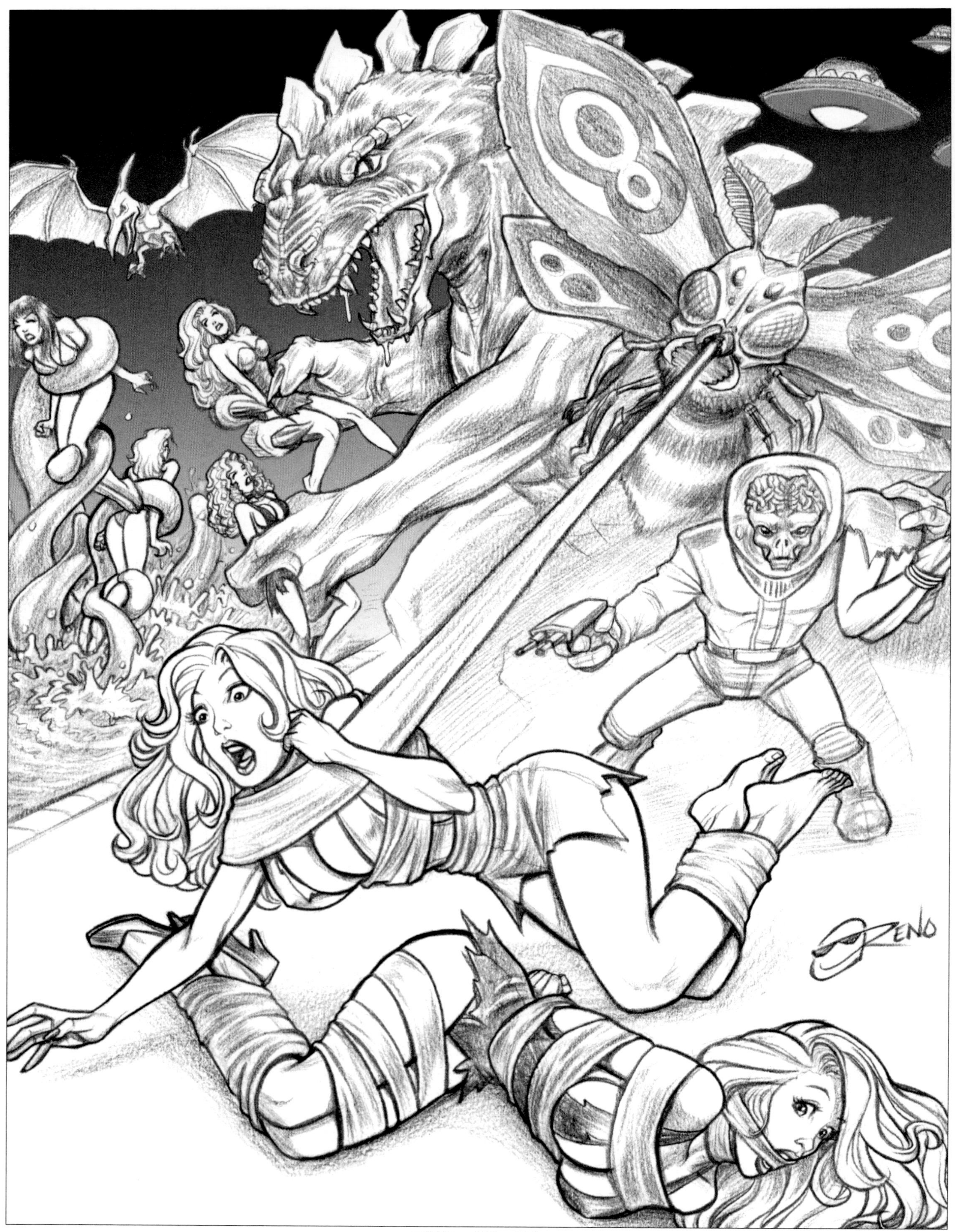

1950's - Killer "B"s

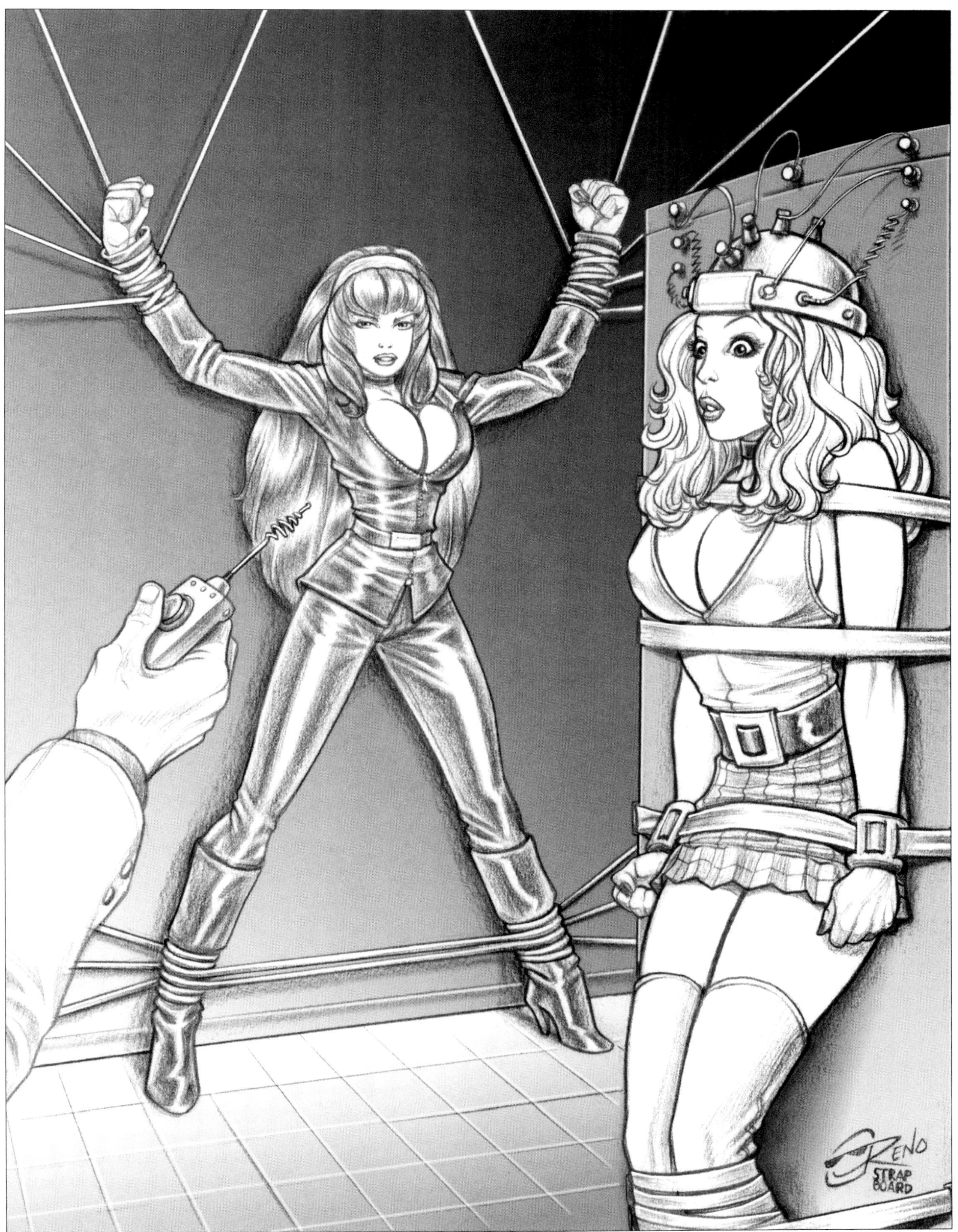

1960's - Spy Girl

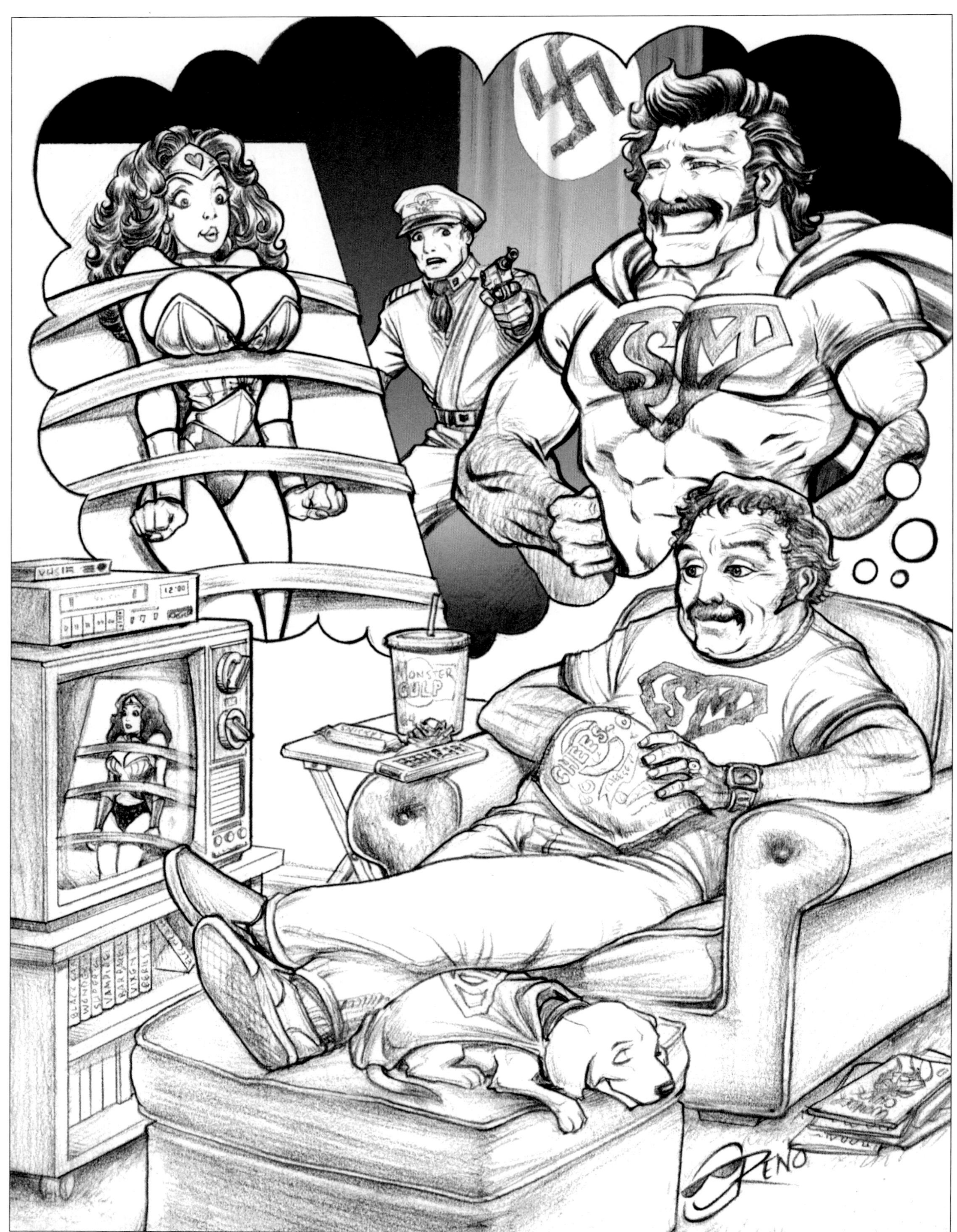

1970's - Armchair Hero

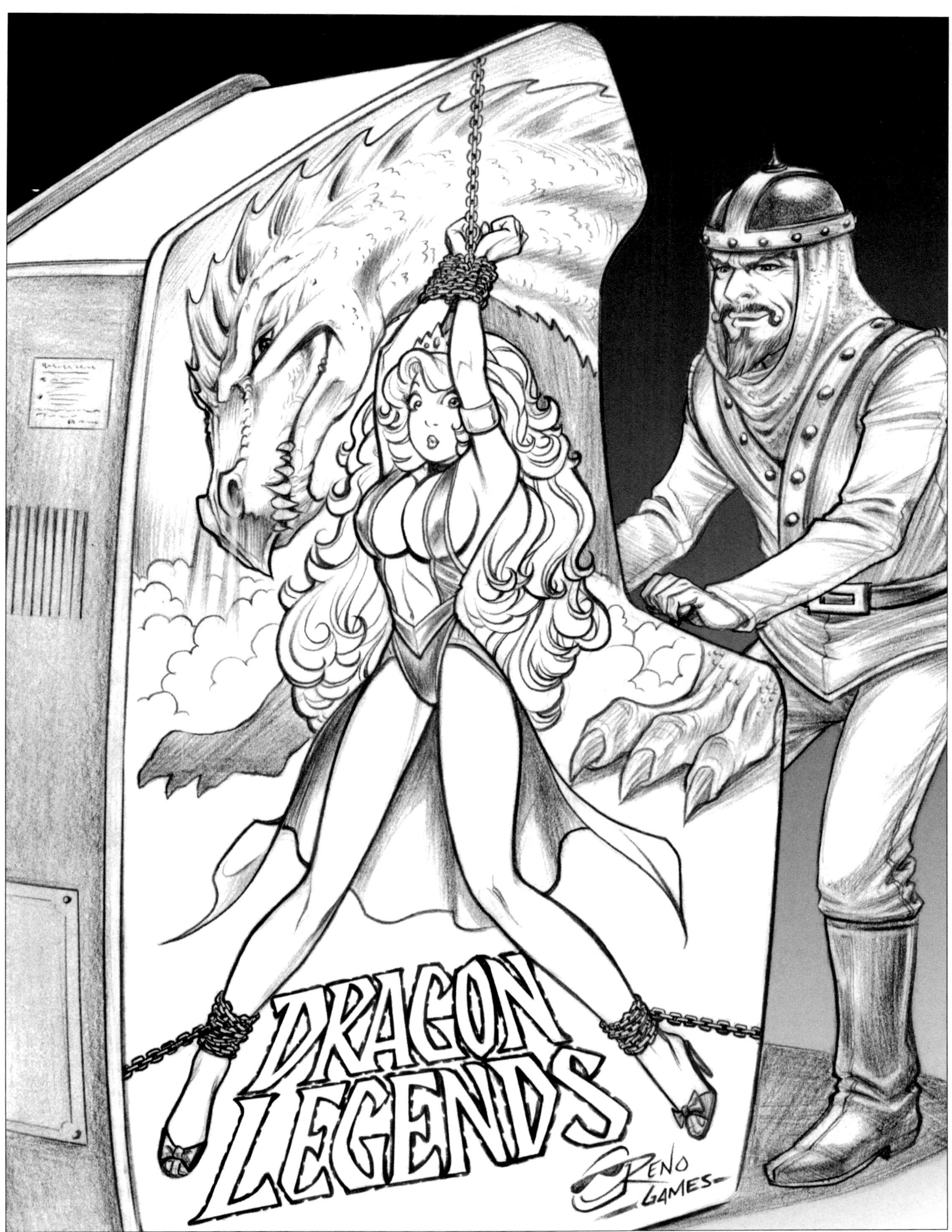

1980's - Rescue the Princess

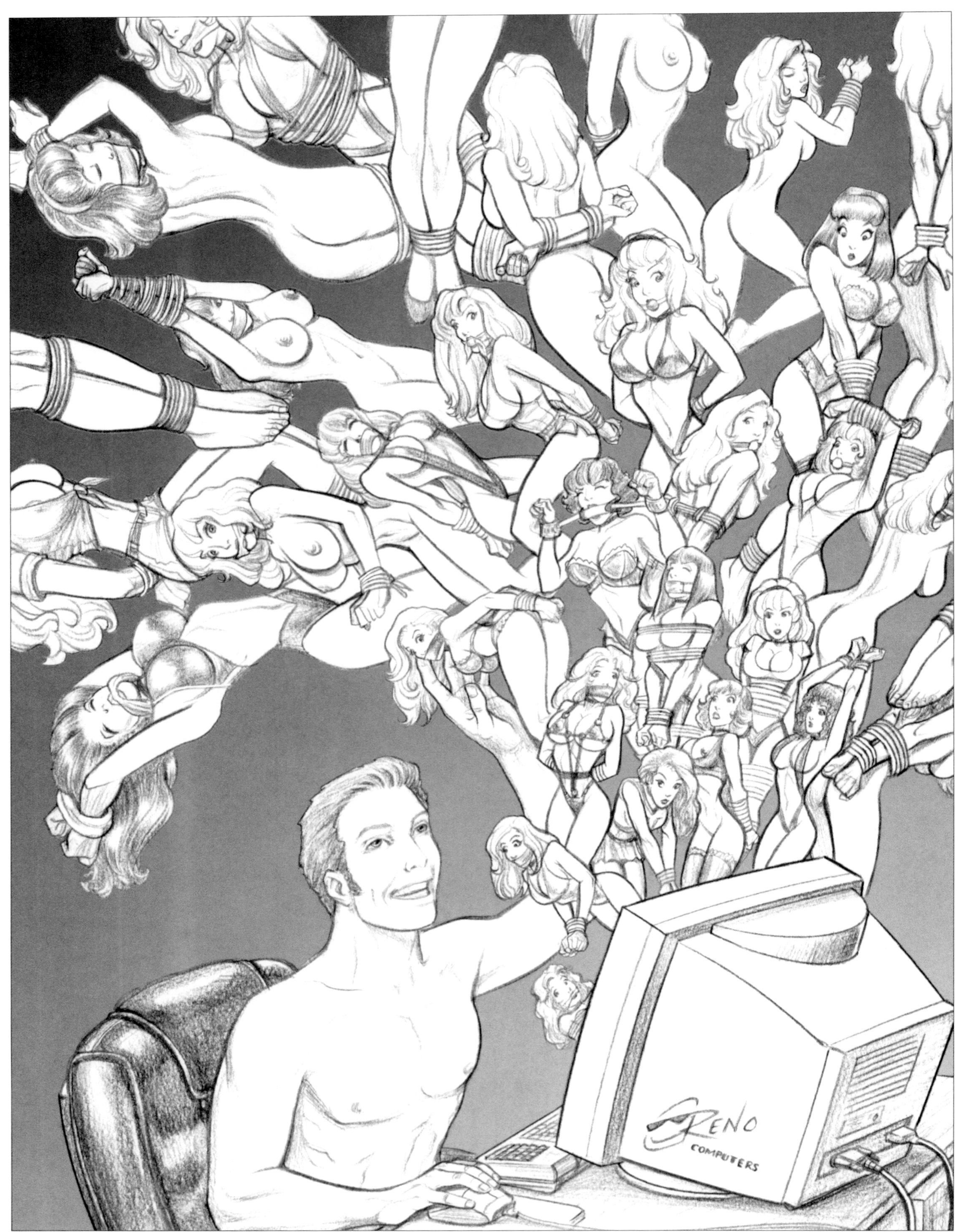

1990's - Caught in the Net

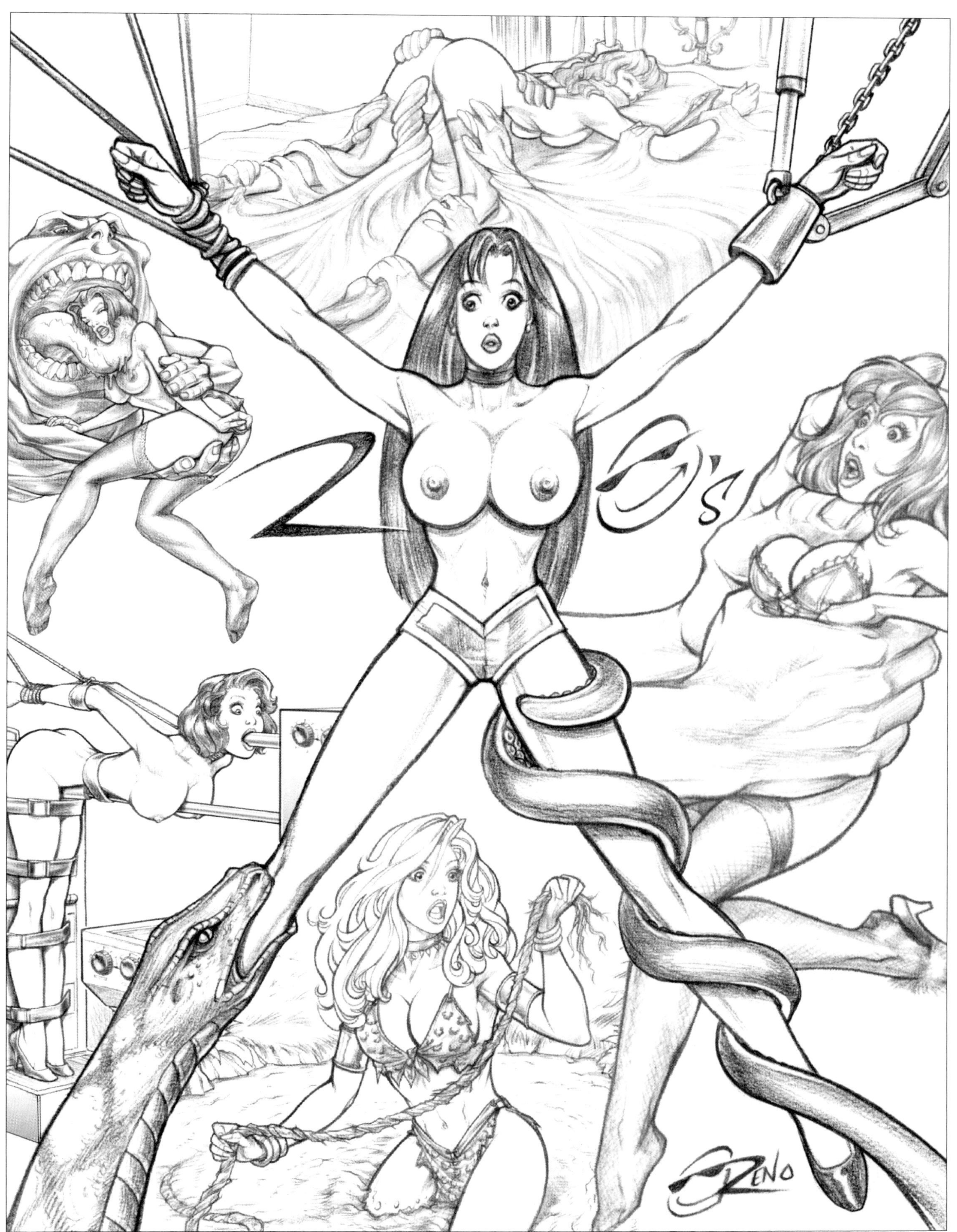

2000's - No Limits

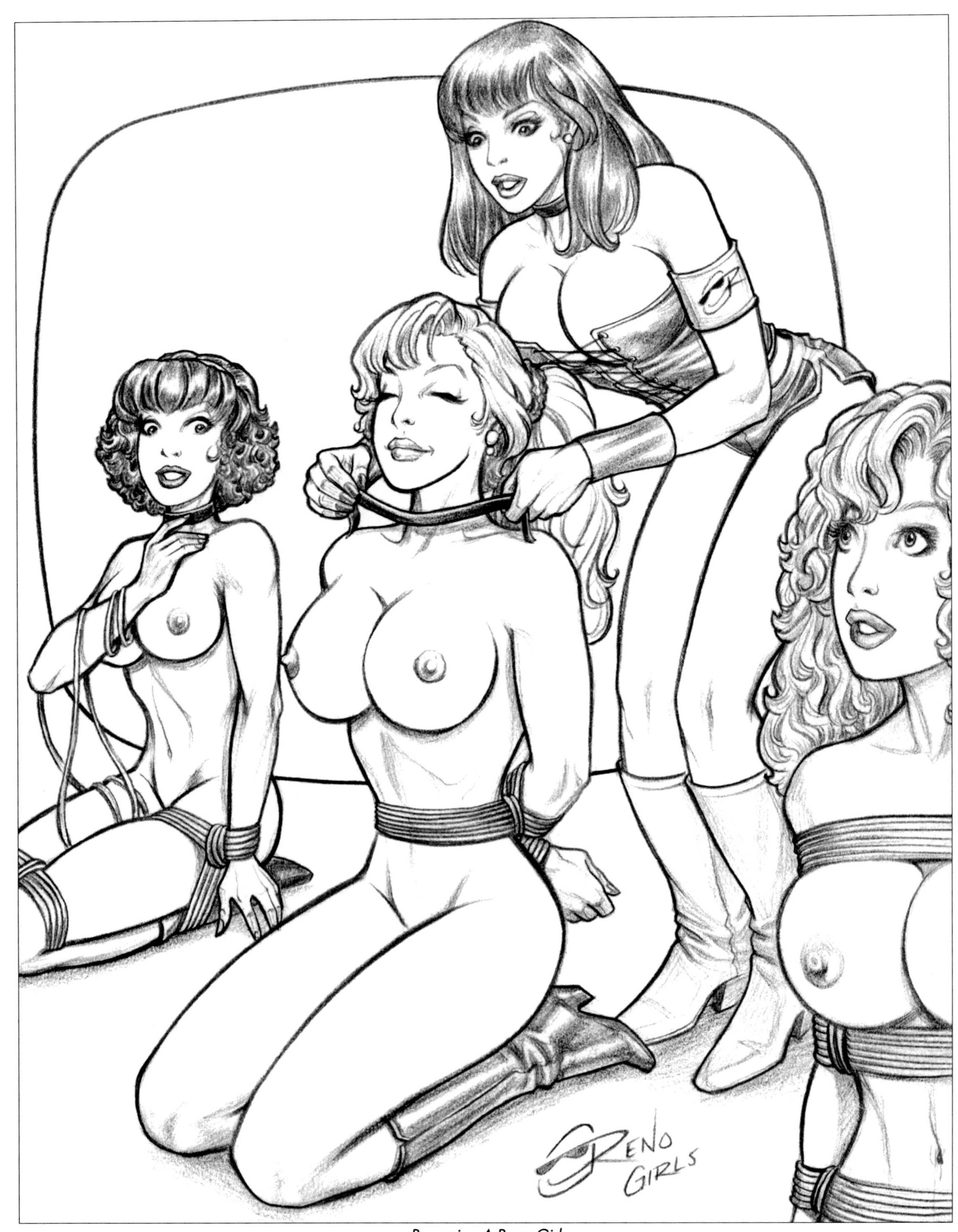

Becoming A Reno Girl

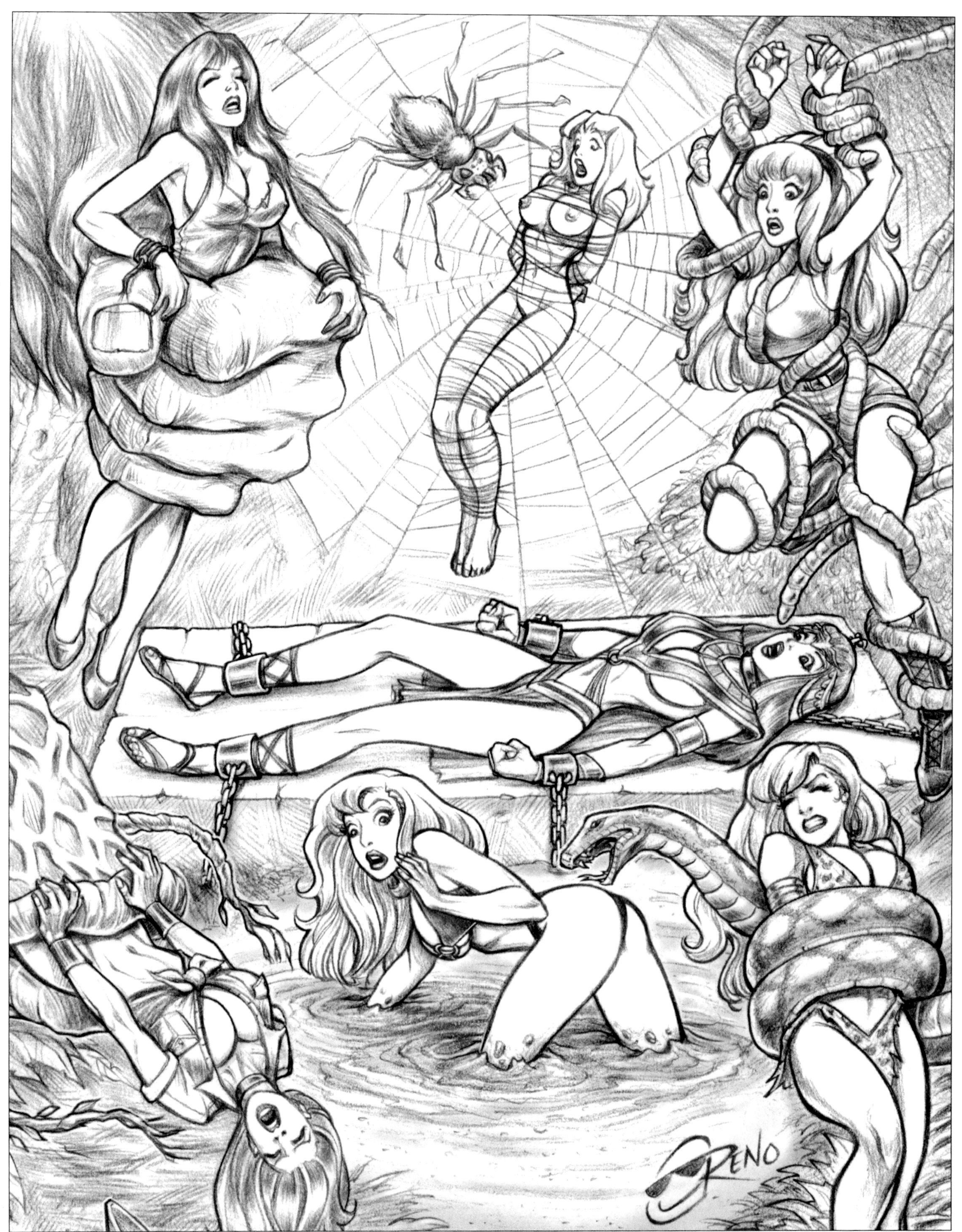

Sensual Distress - The Seven Deadly Sin-suals

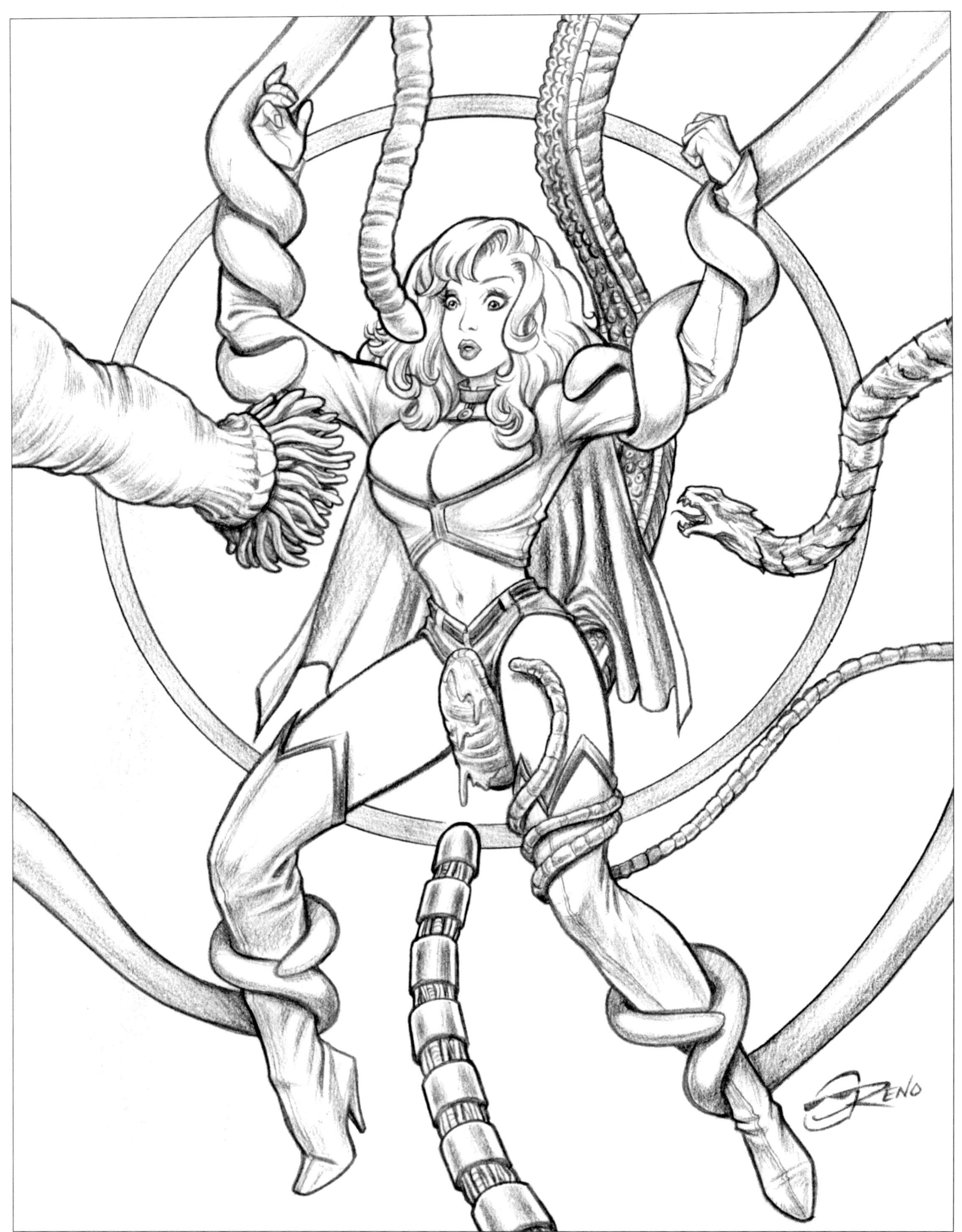

10-tacles

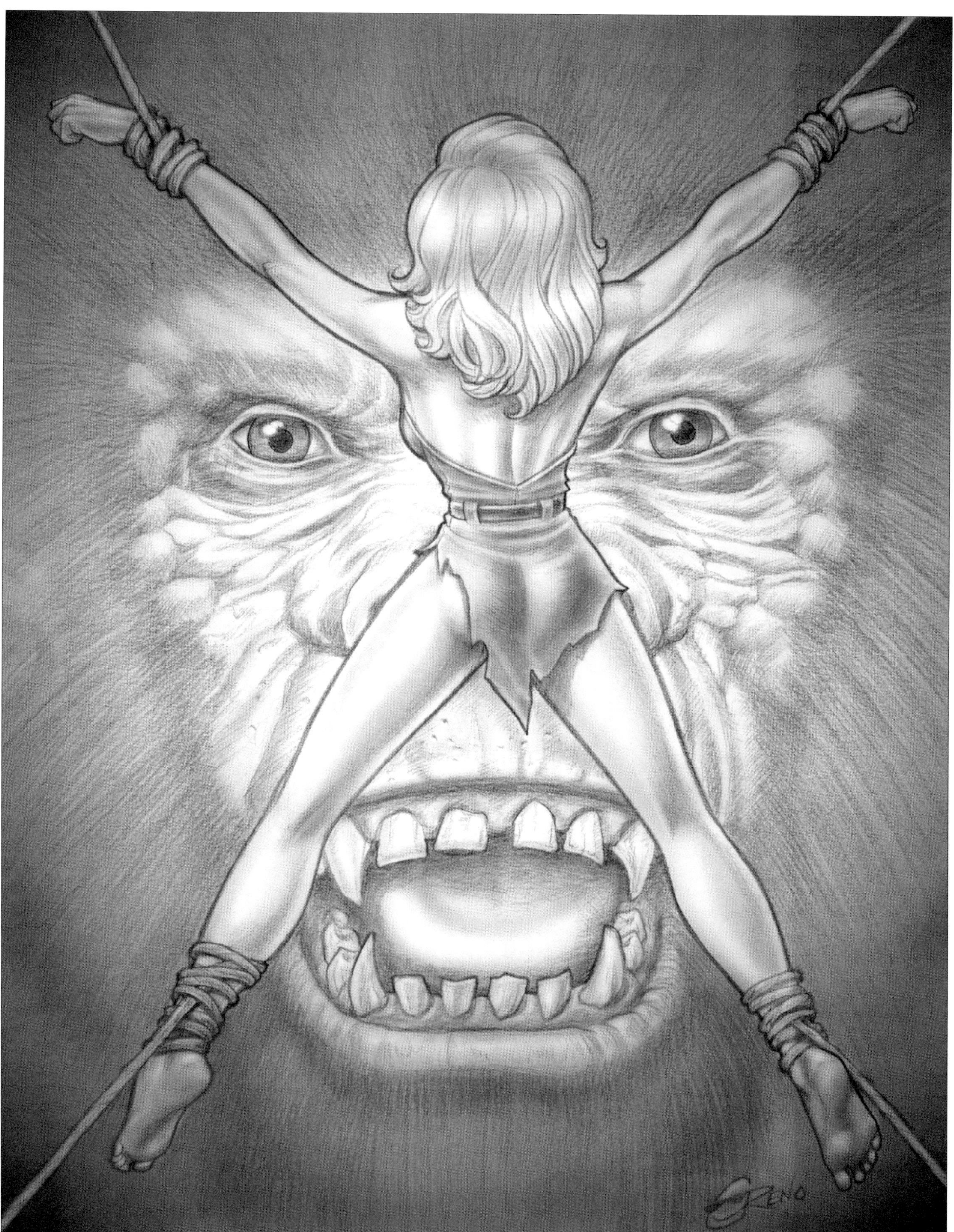

Gorilla My Dreams

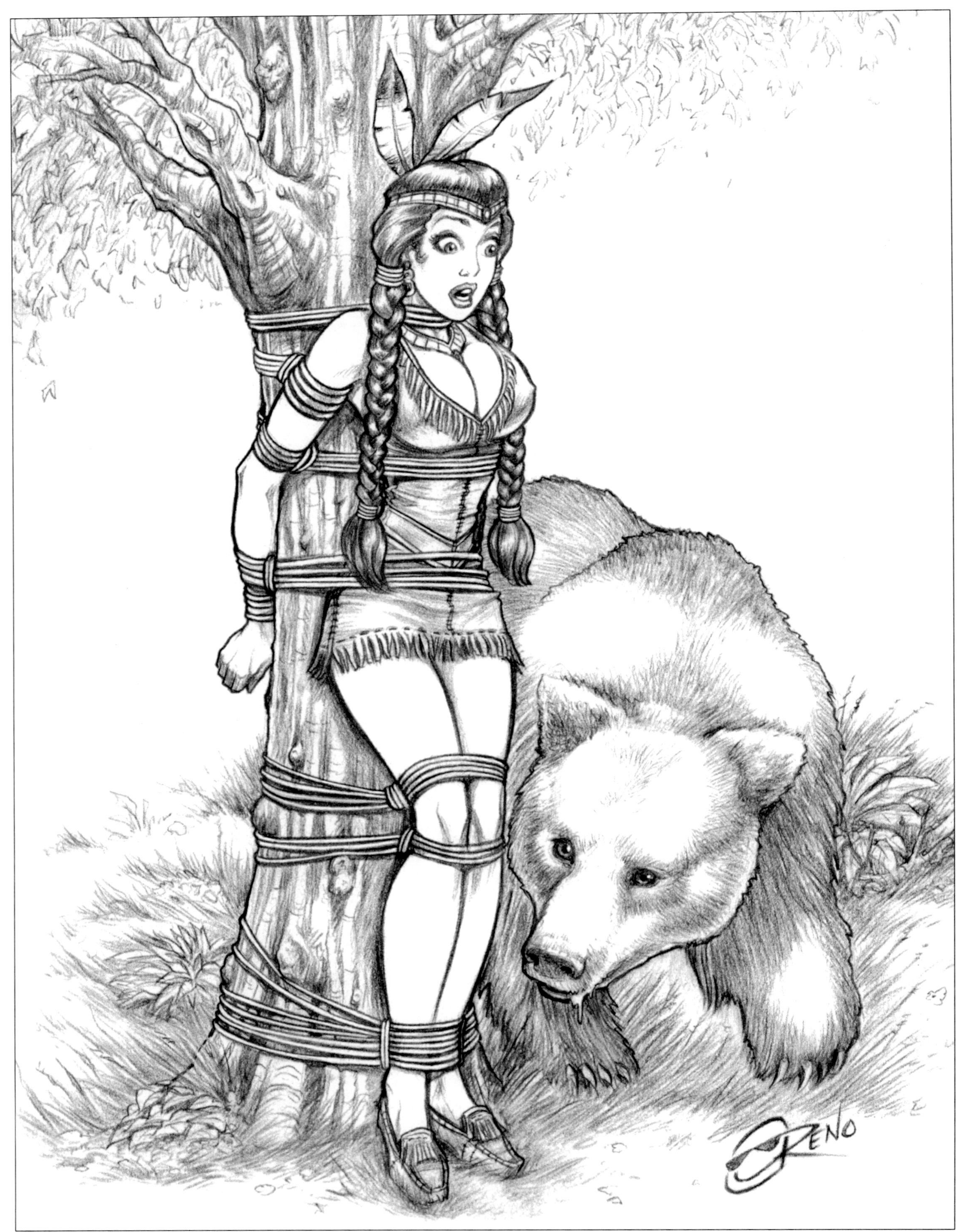

Indian Food

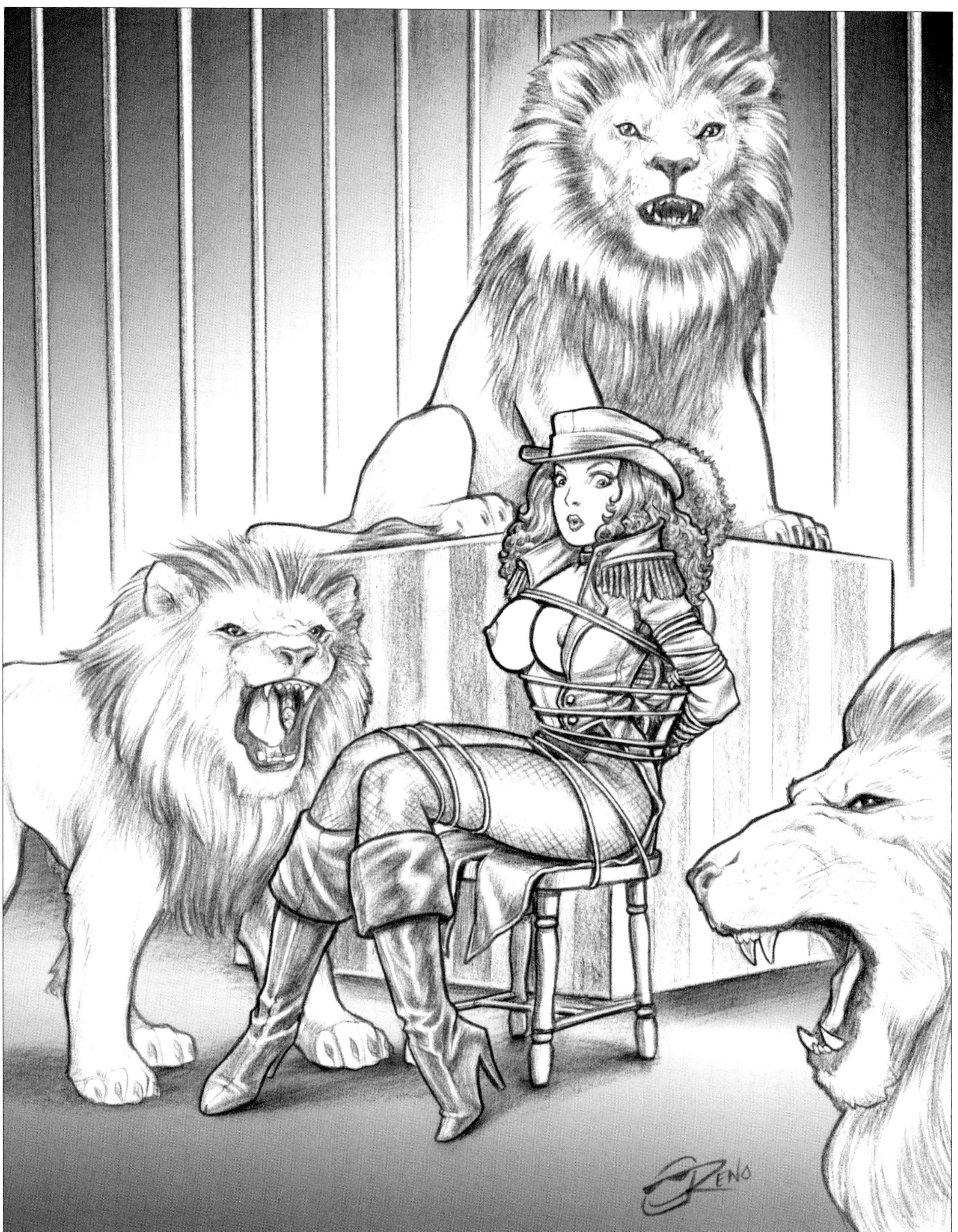

Lion Tamer

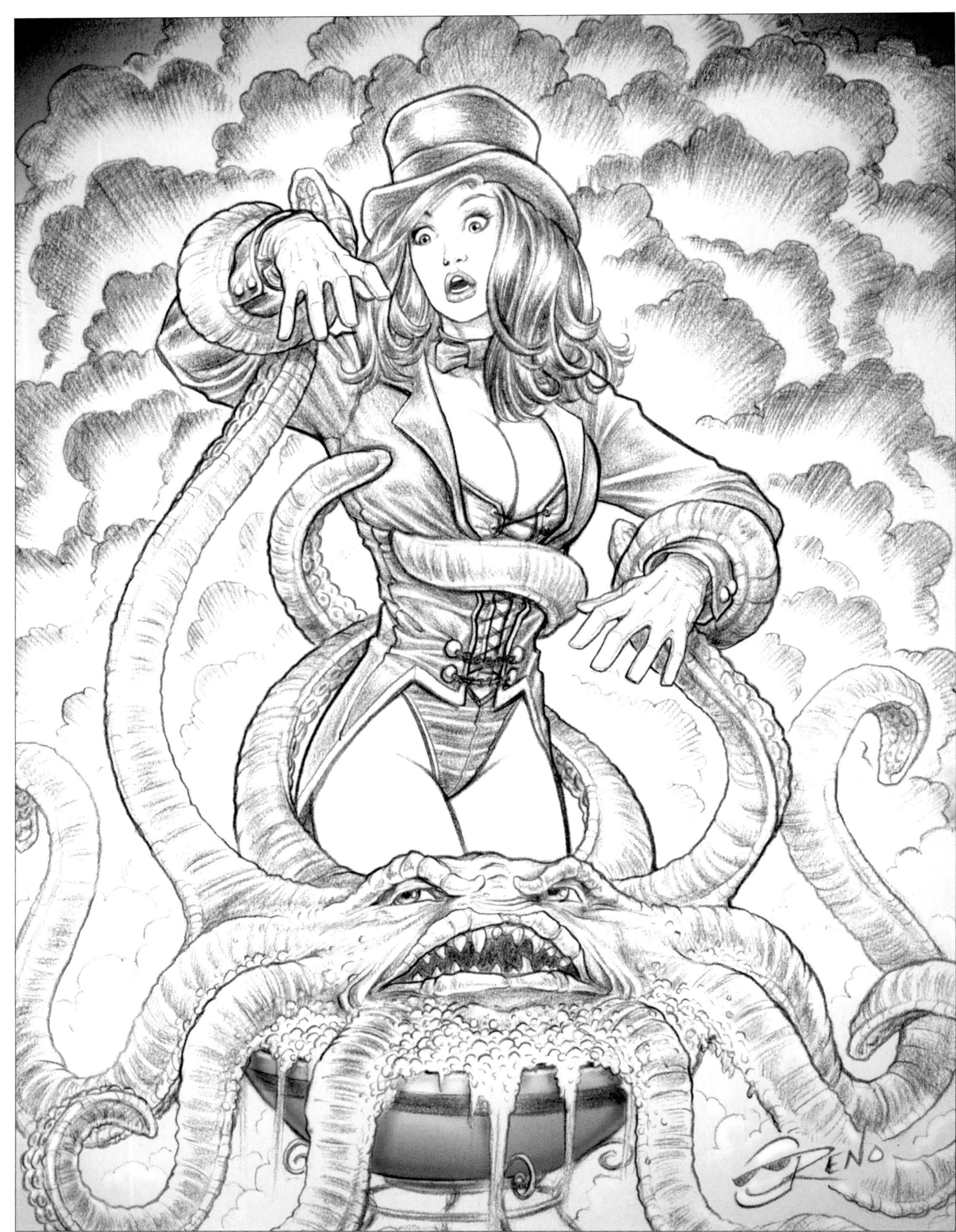

Magician's Assistant

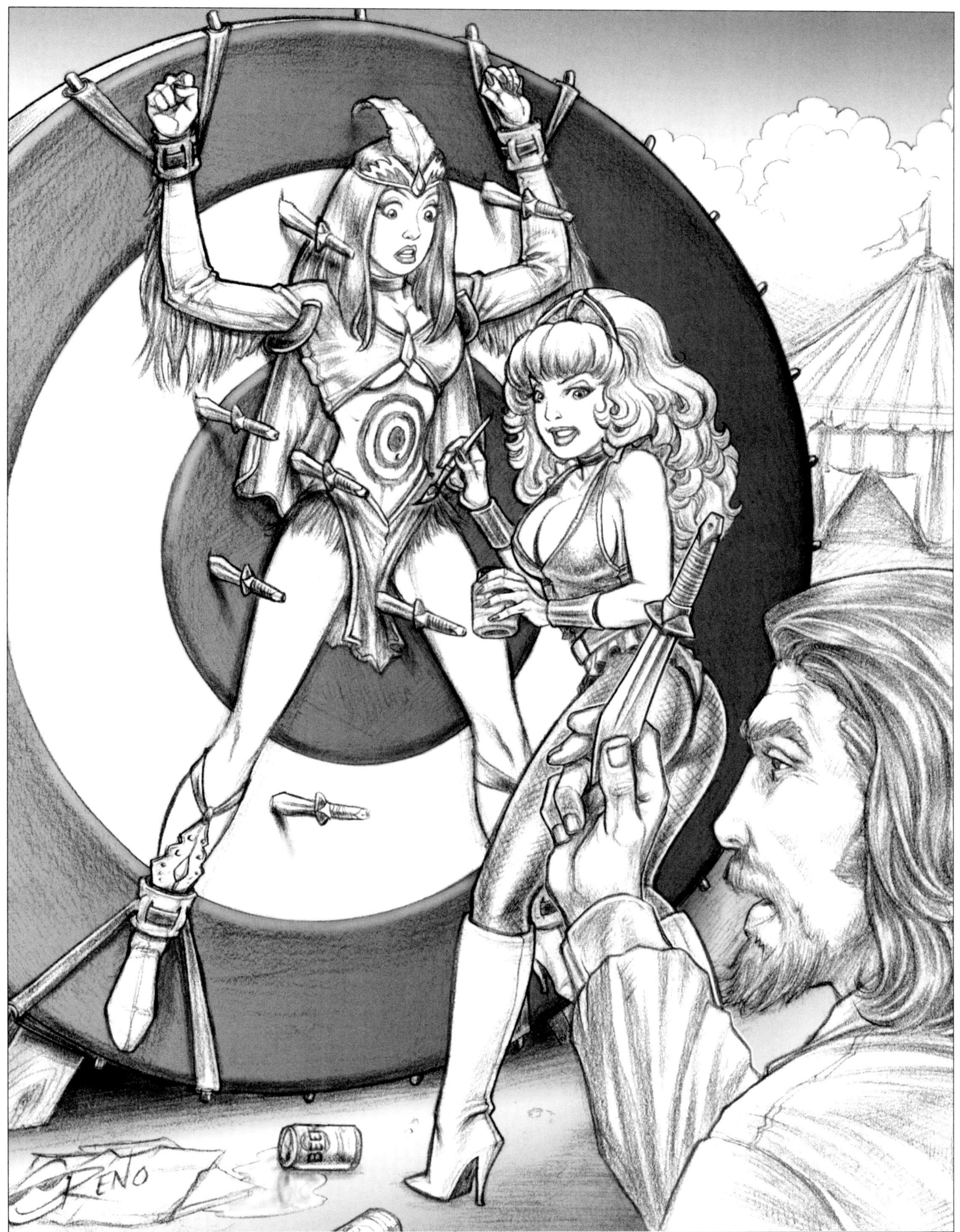

Drunk Kniving

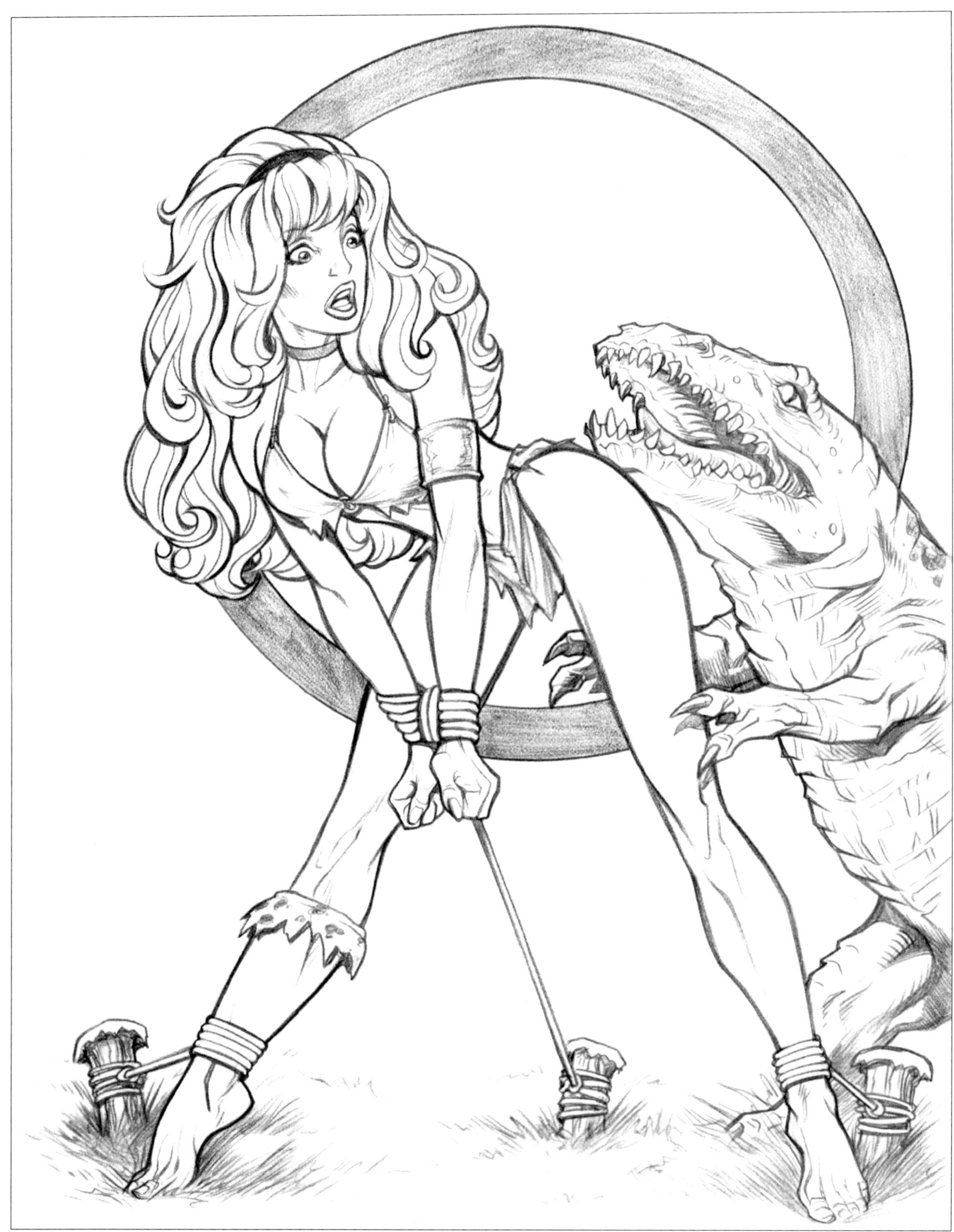

DinoGator

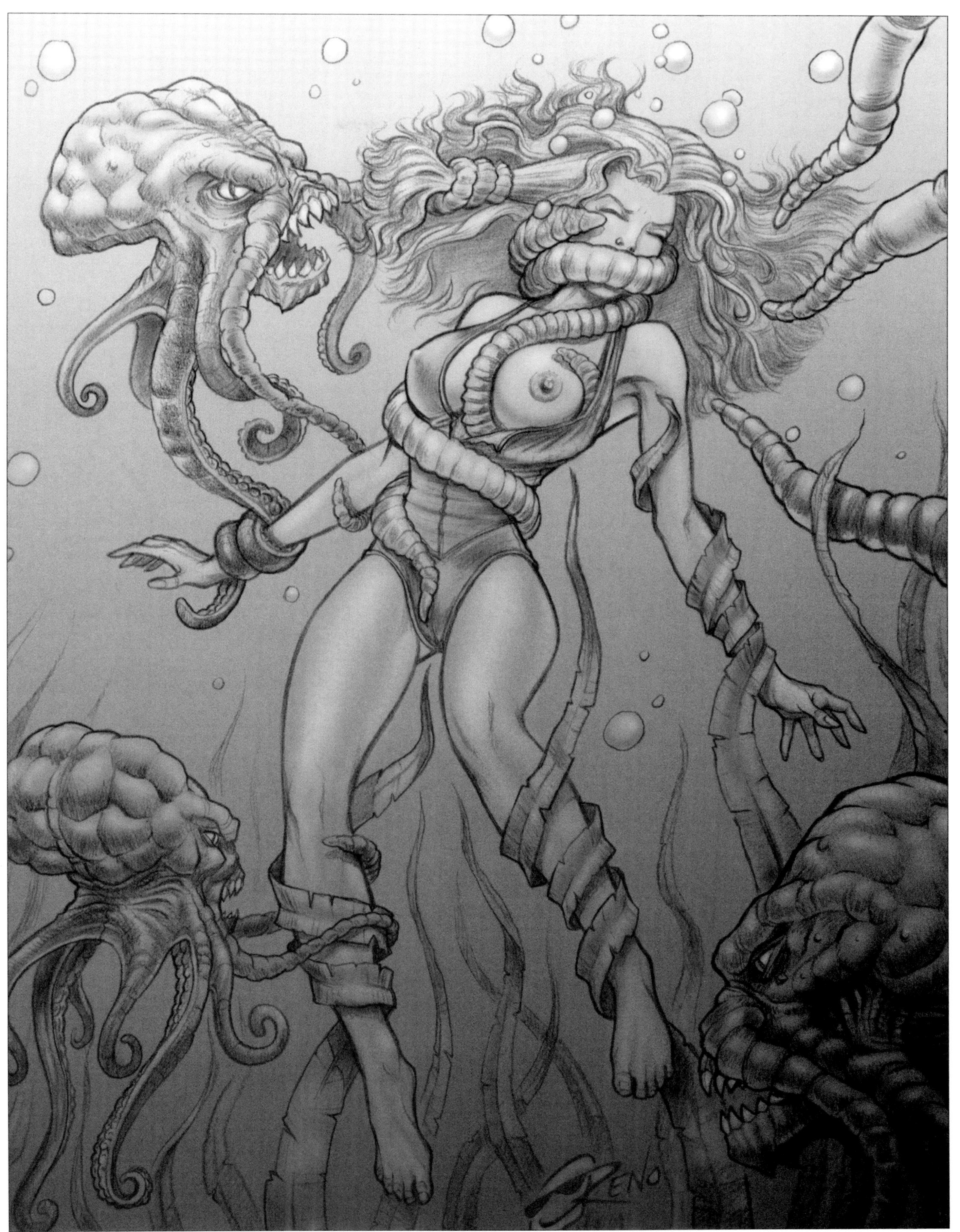

Currently Octopied

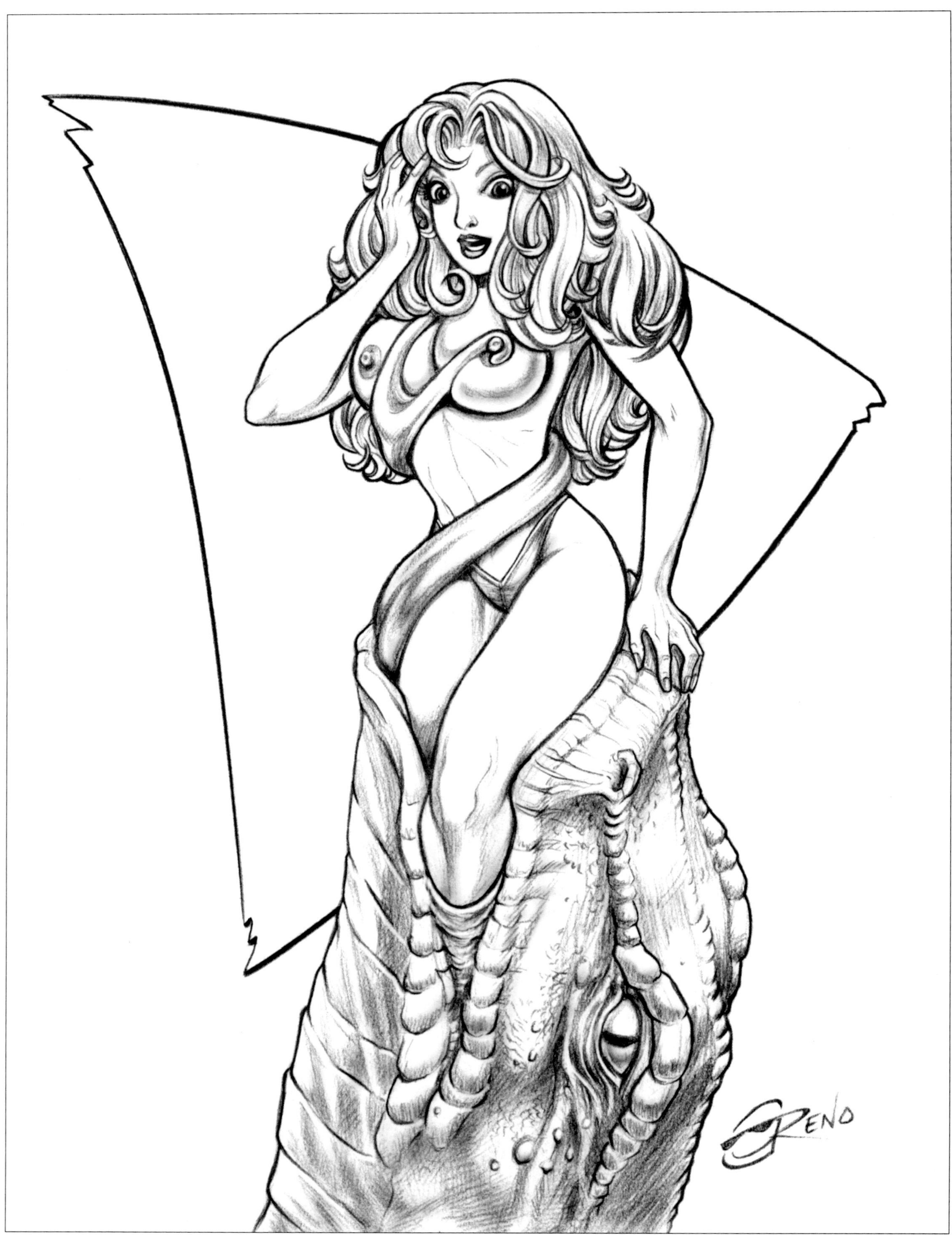

Snake Charmer

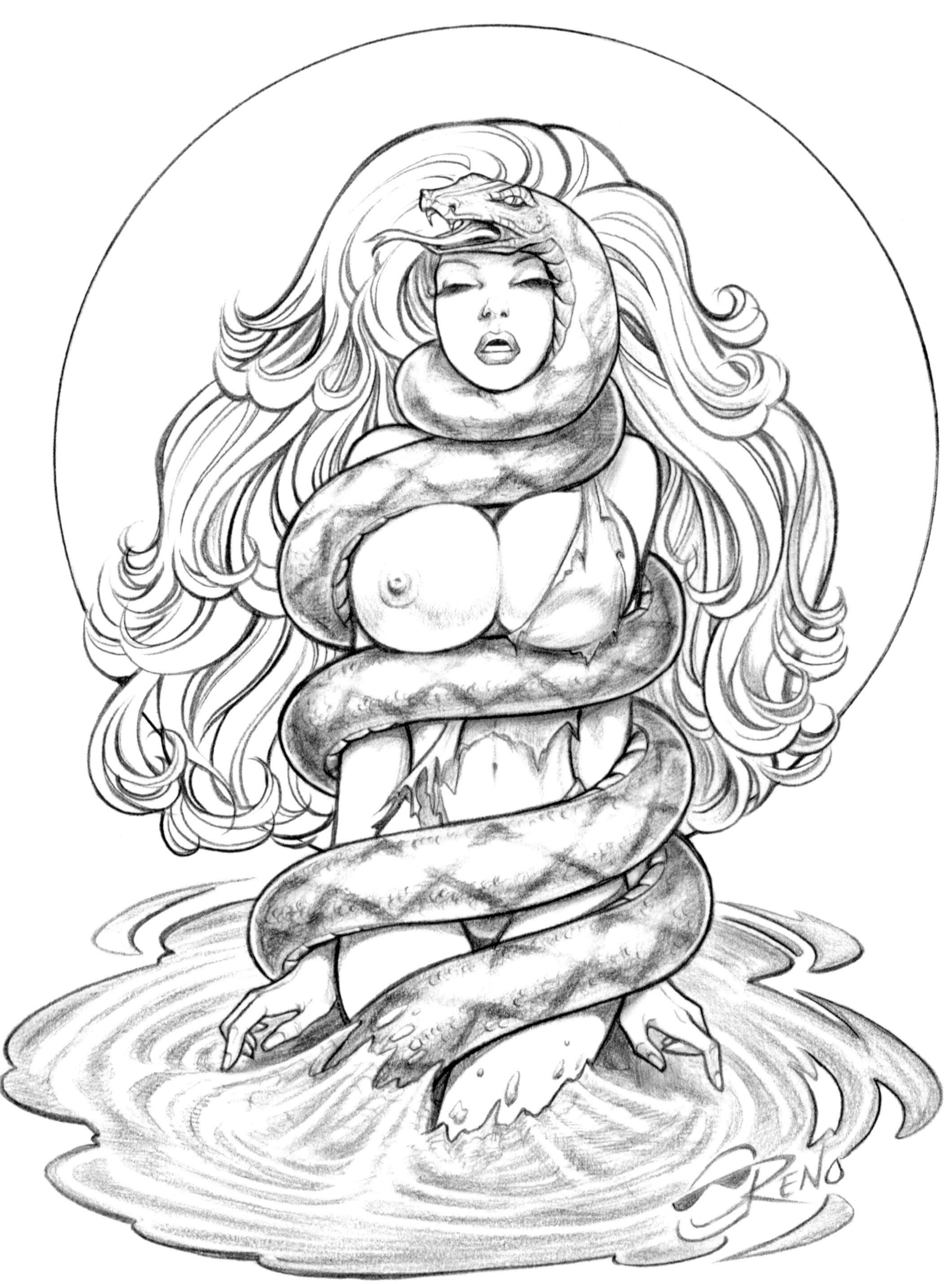

Quicksand Snake

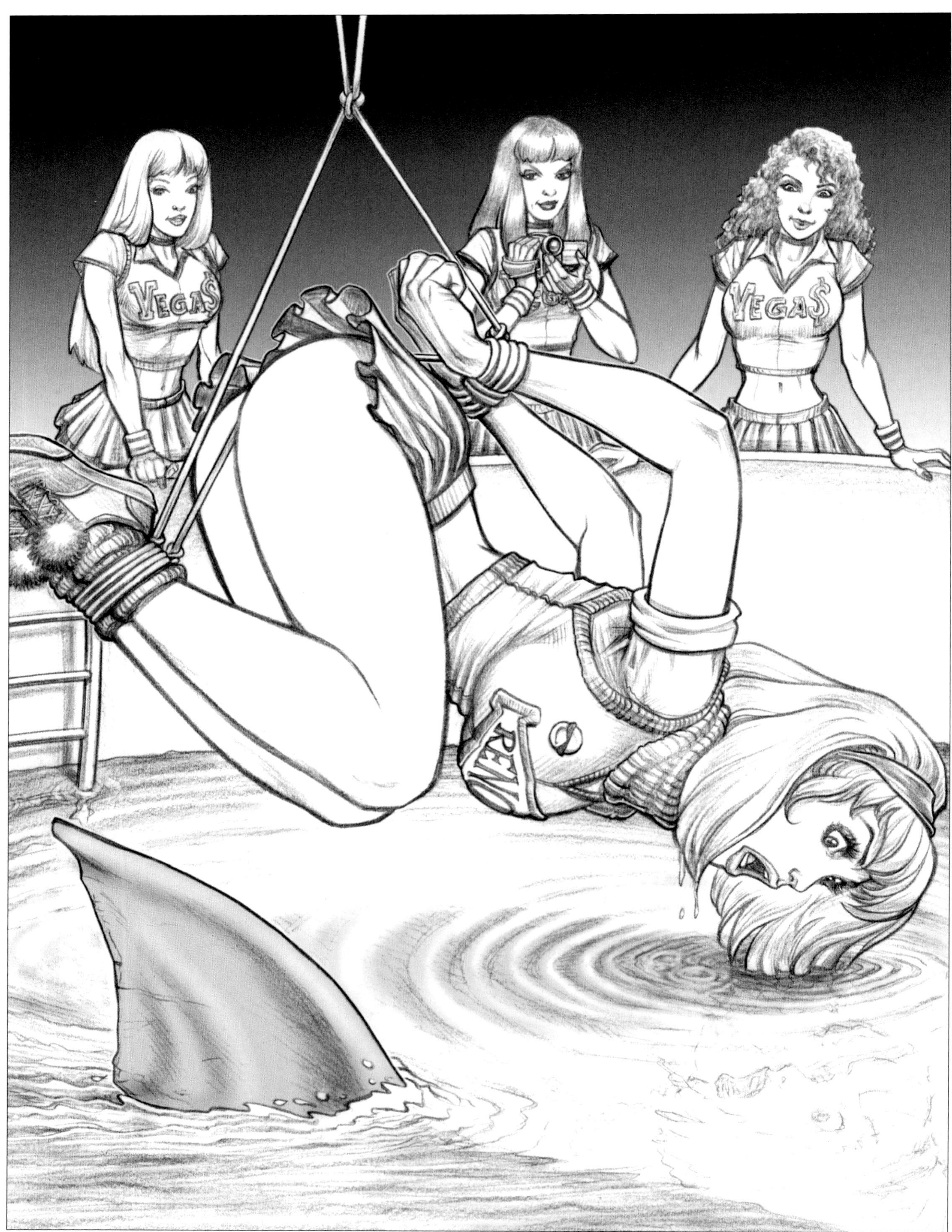

Pool Sharks

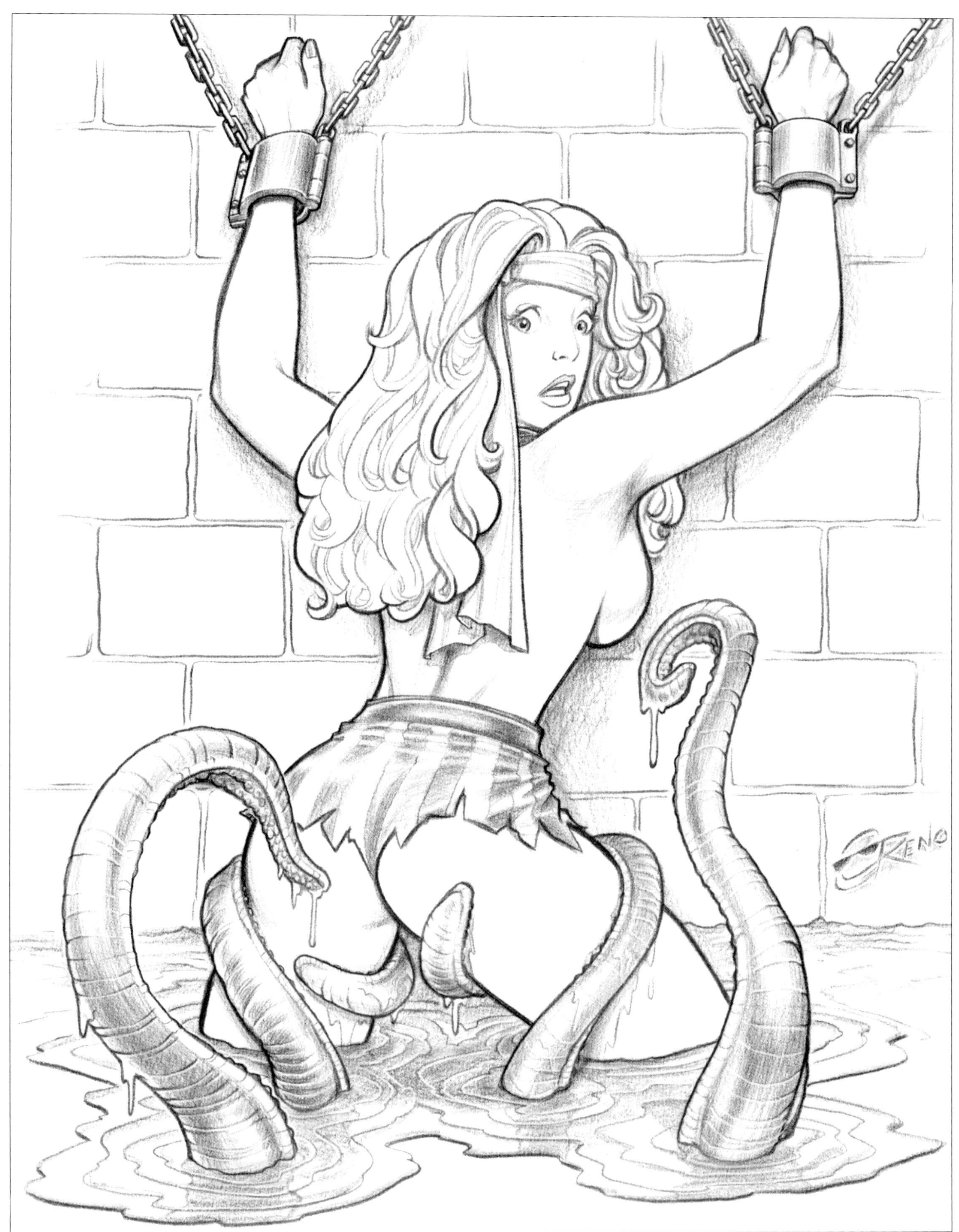

Plundering the Booty

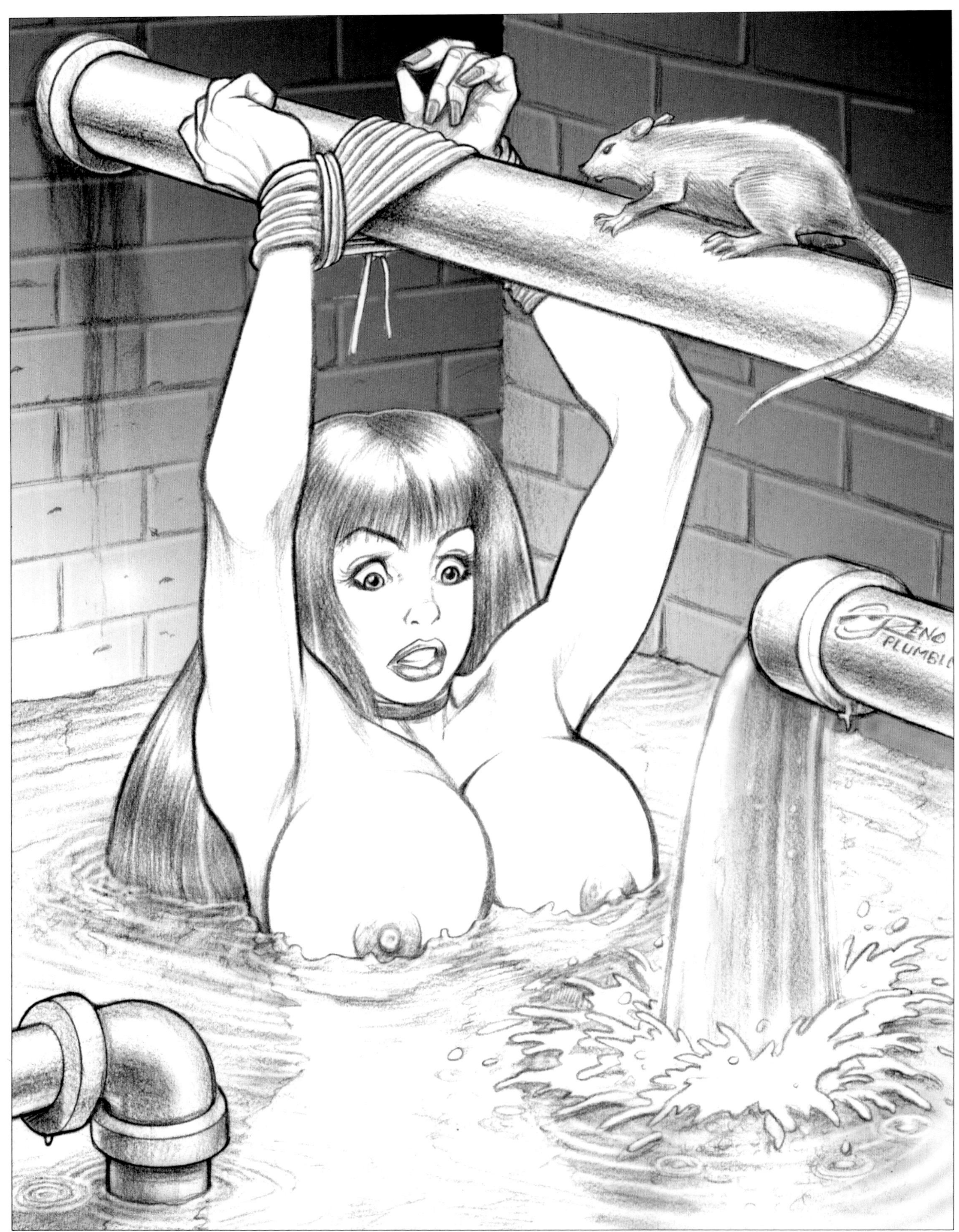

Sewer Treatment

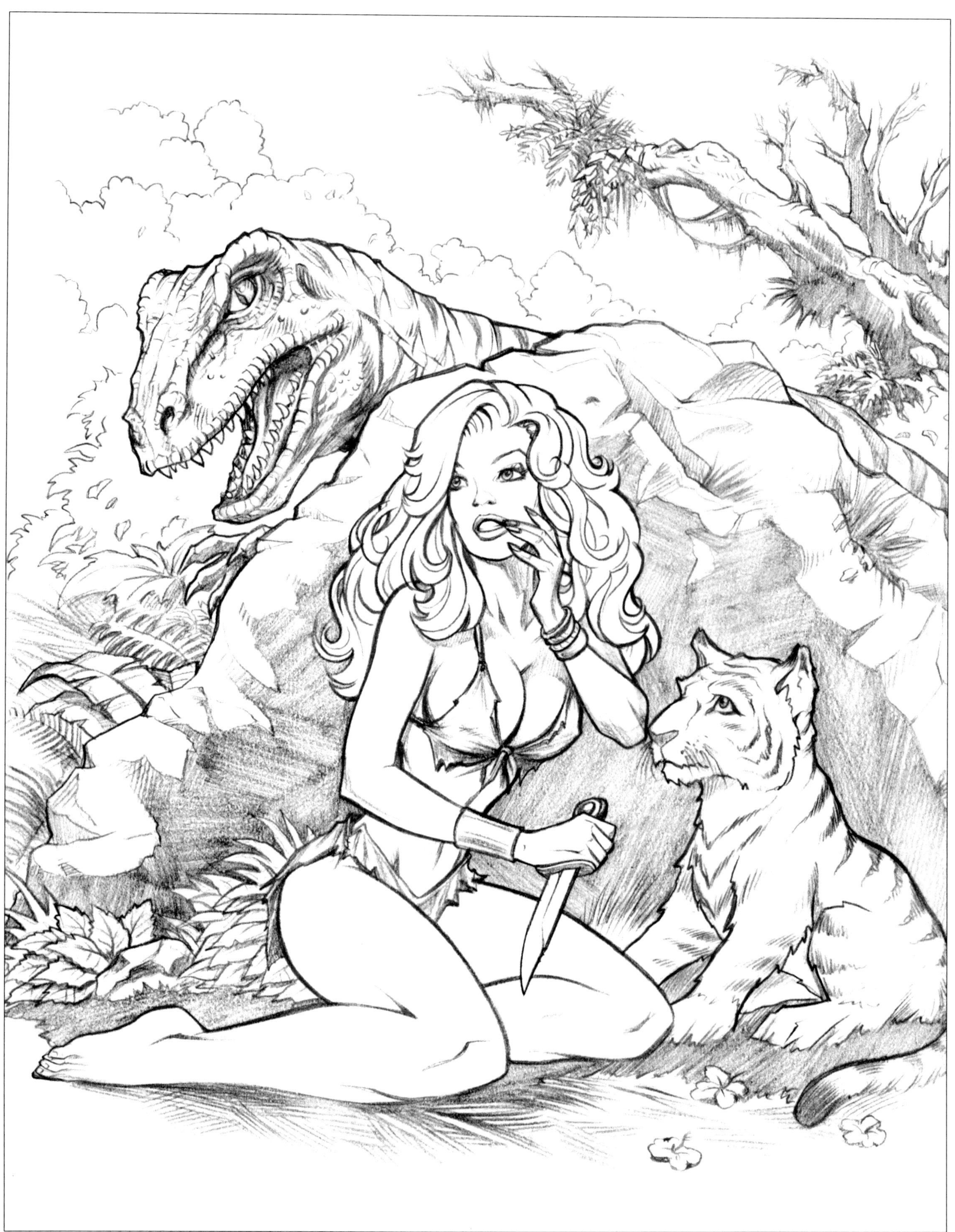

The Tigress

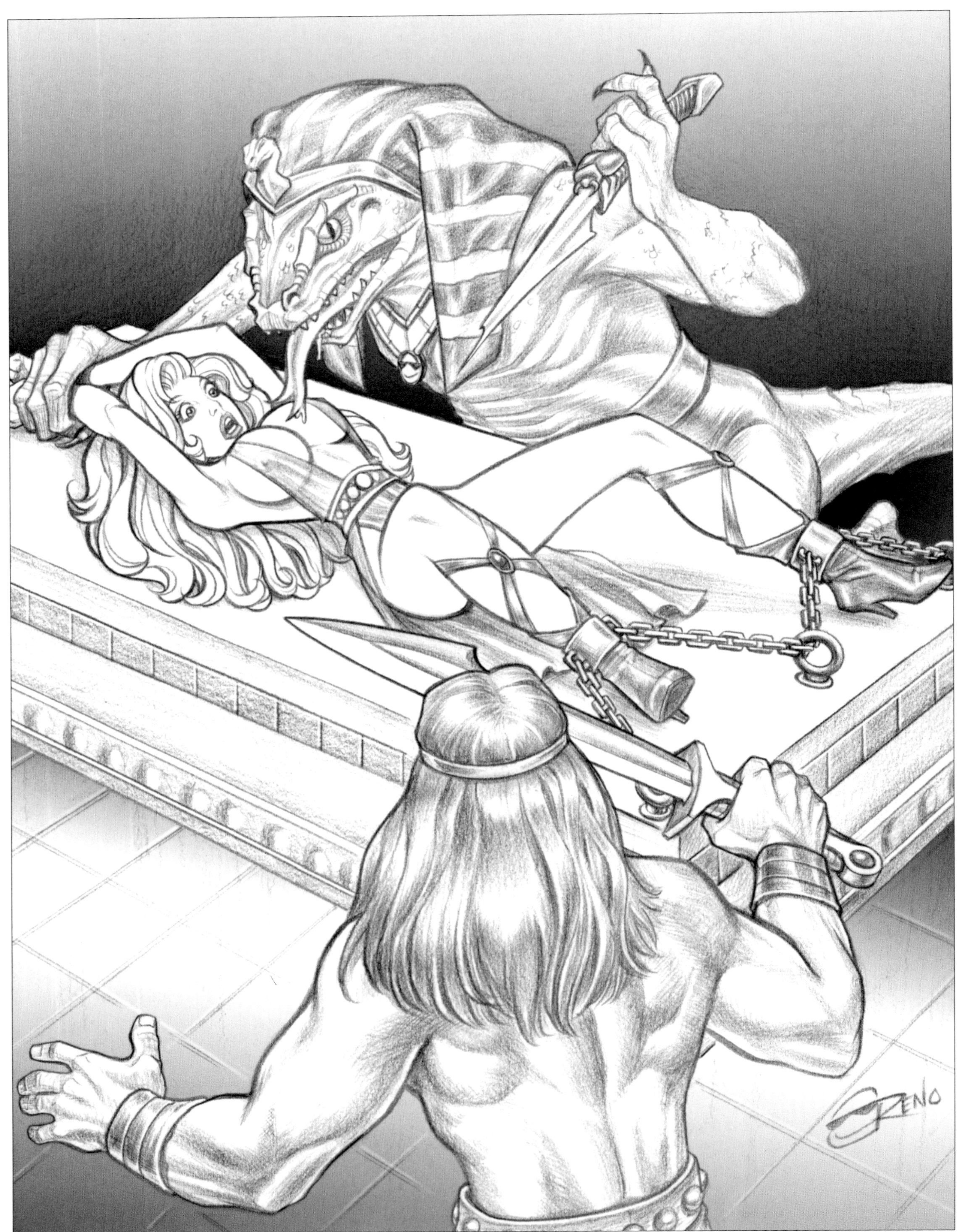

Lizard King

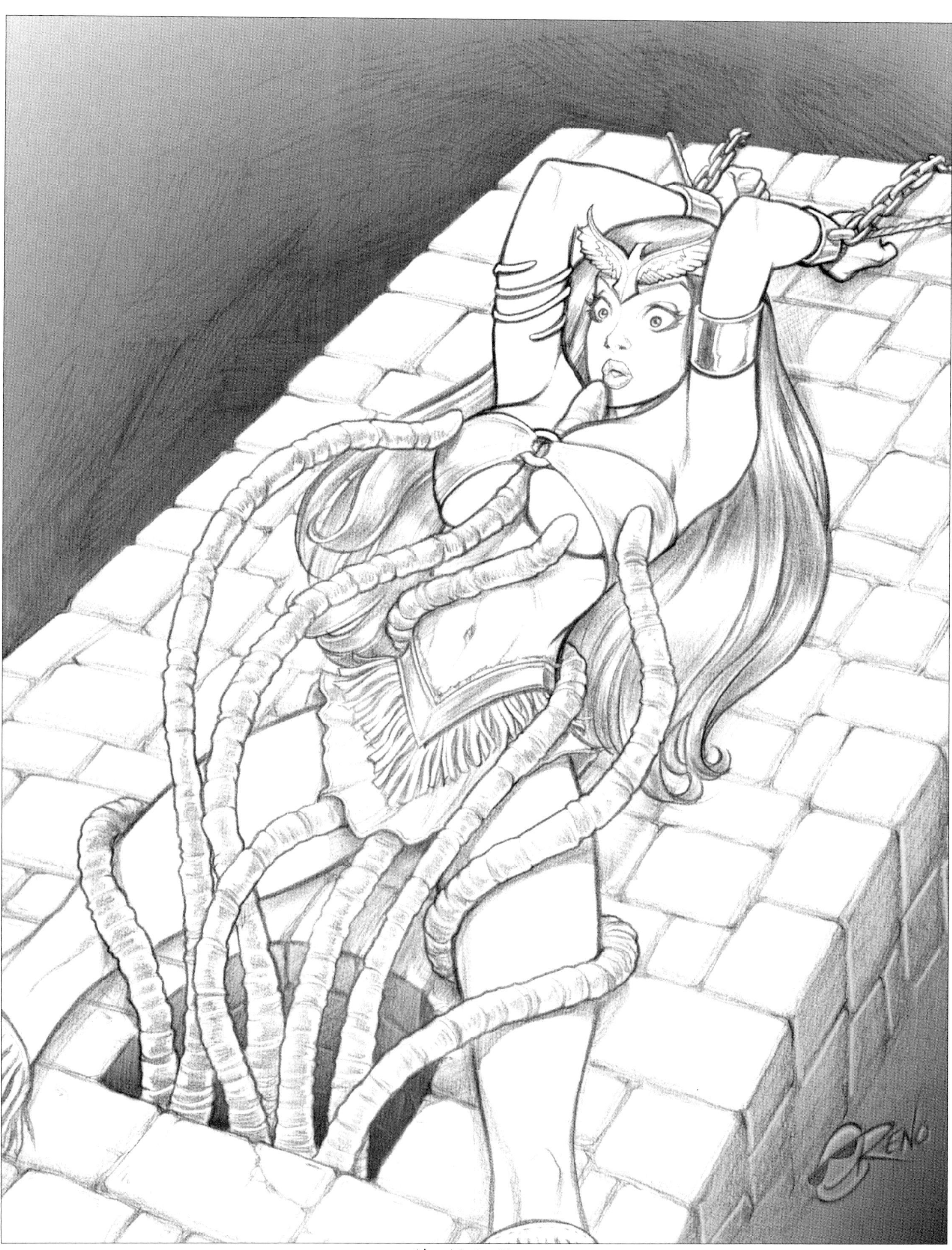

Altar Native Tastes

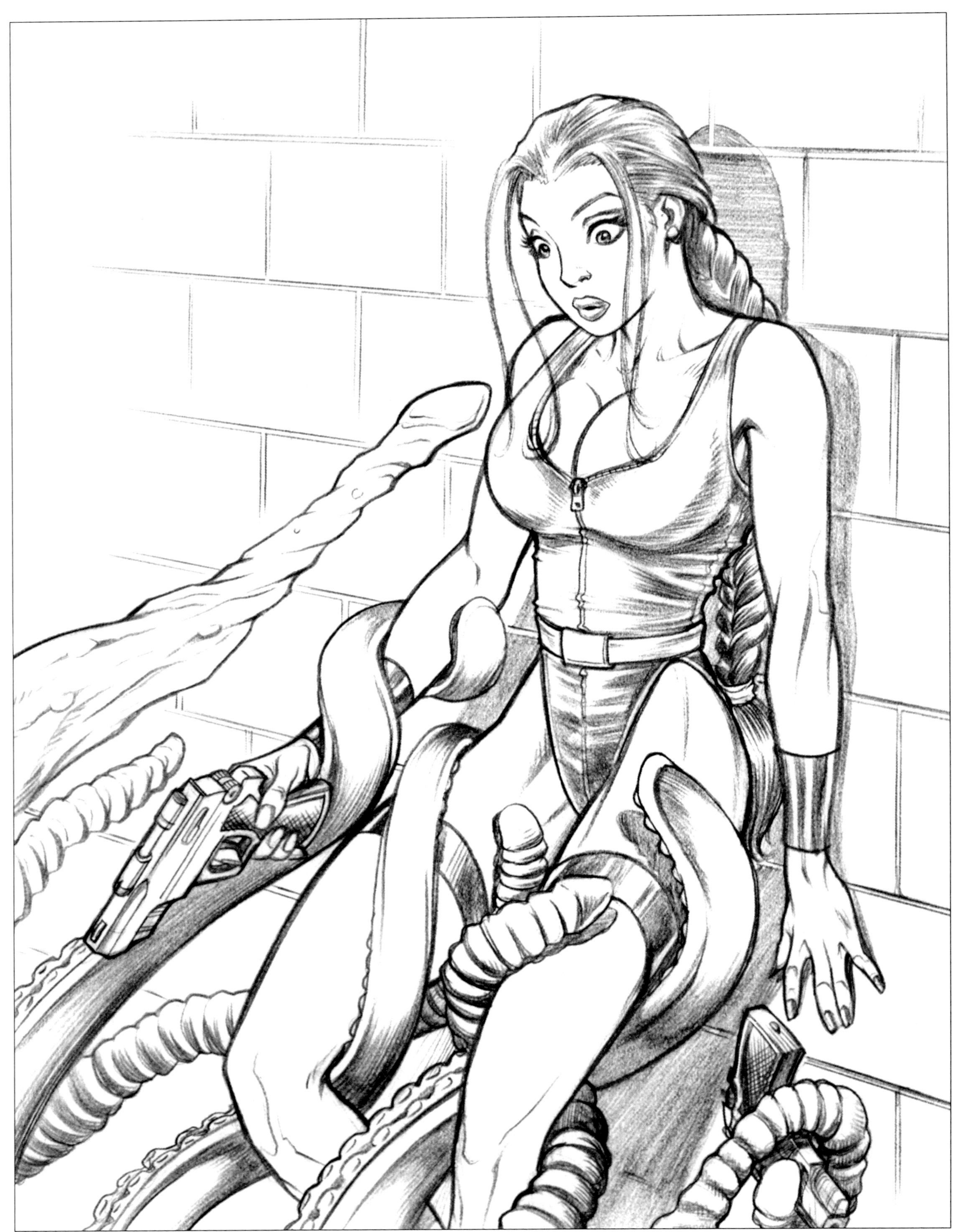

X-Plorers

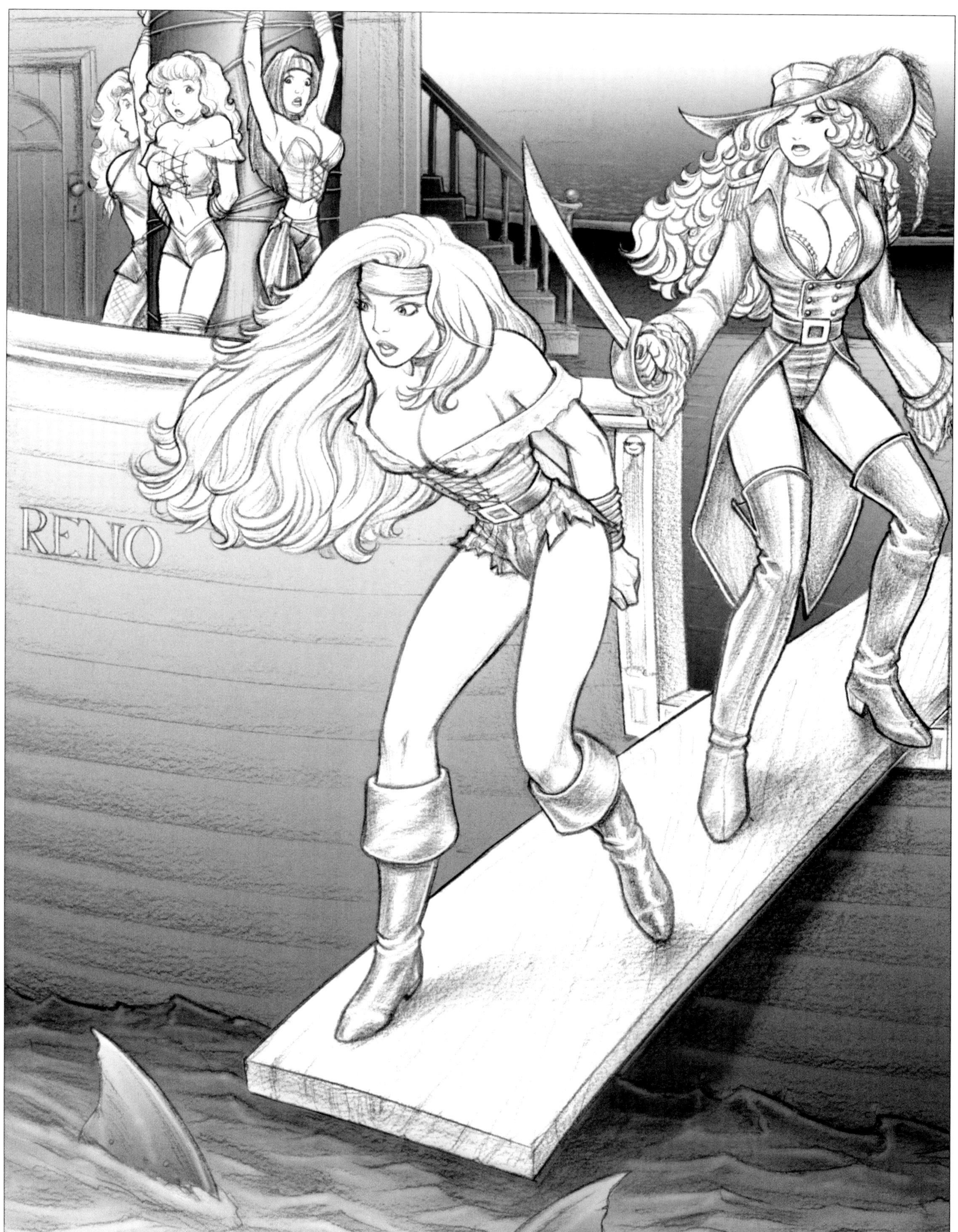

The Longest Yarrrrrrrd

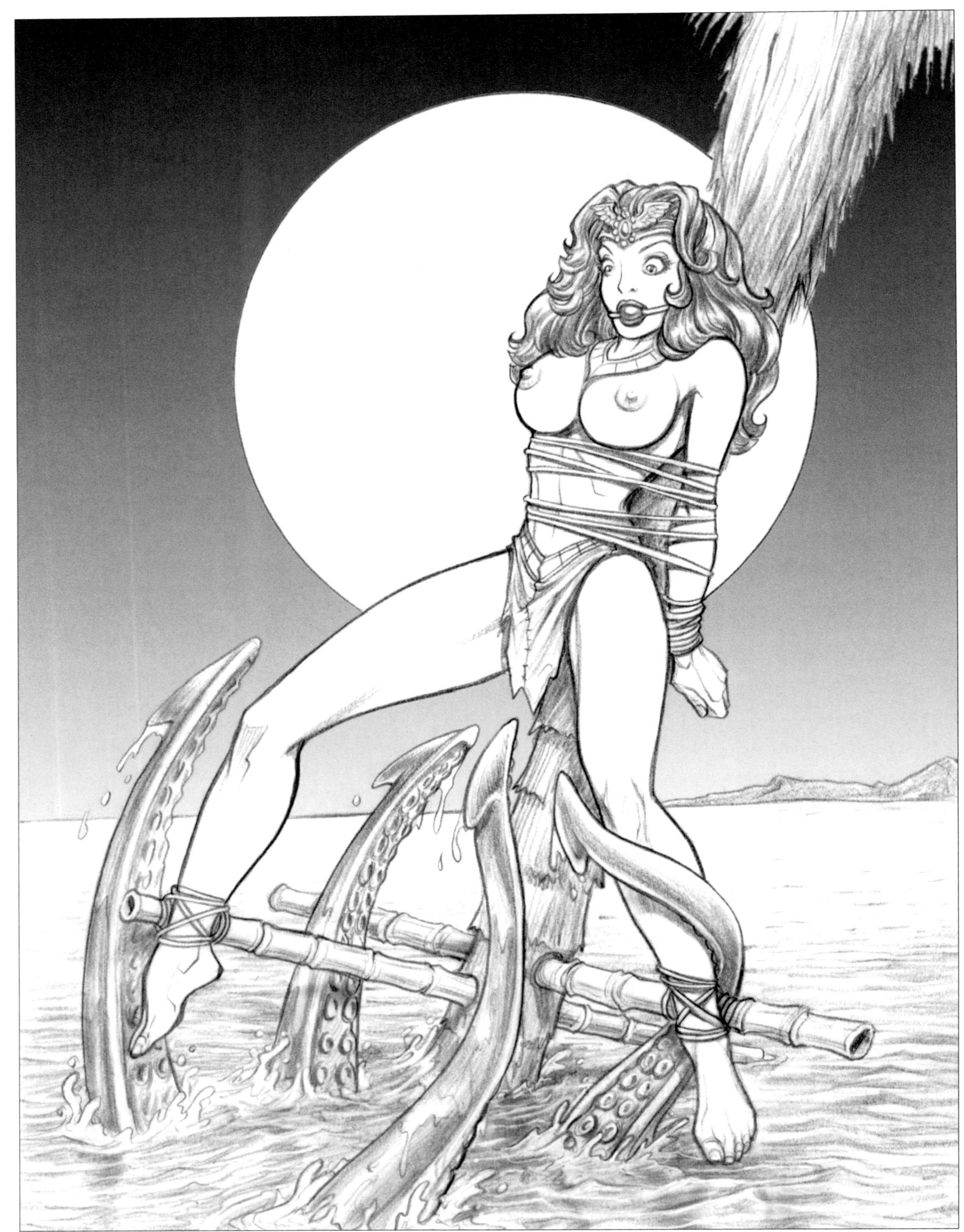

Island Sacrifice

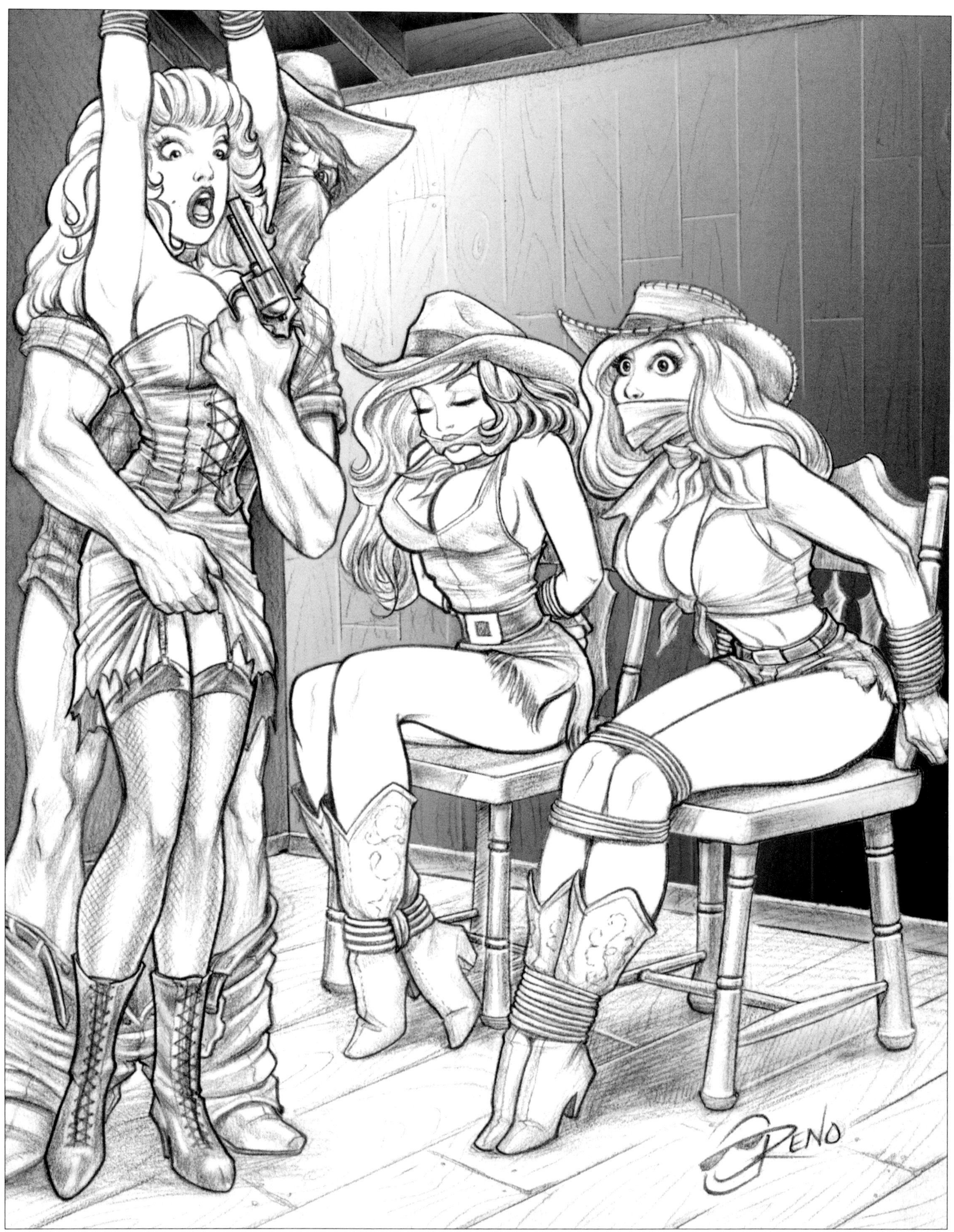

Ride 'em Cowgirls

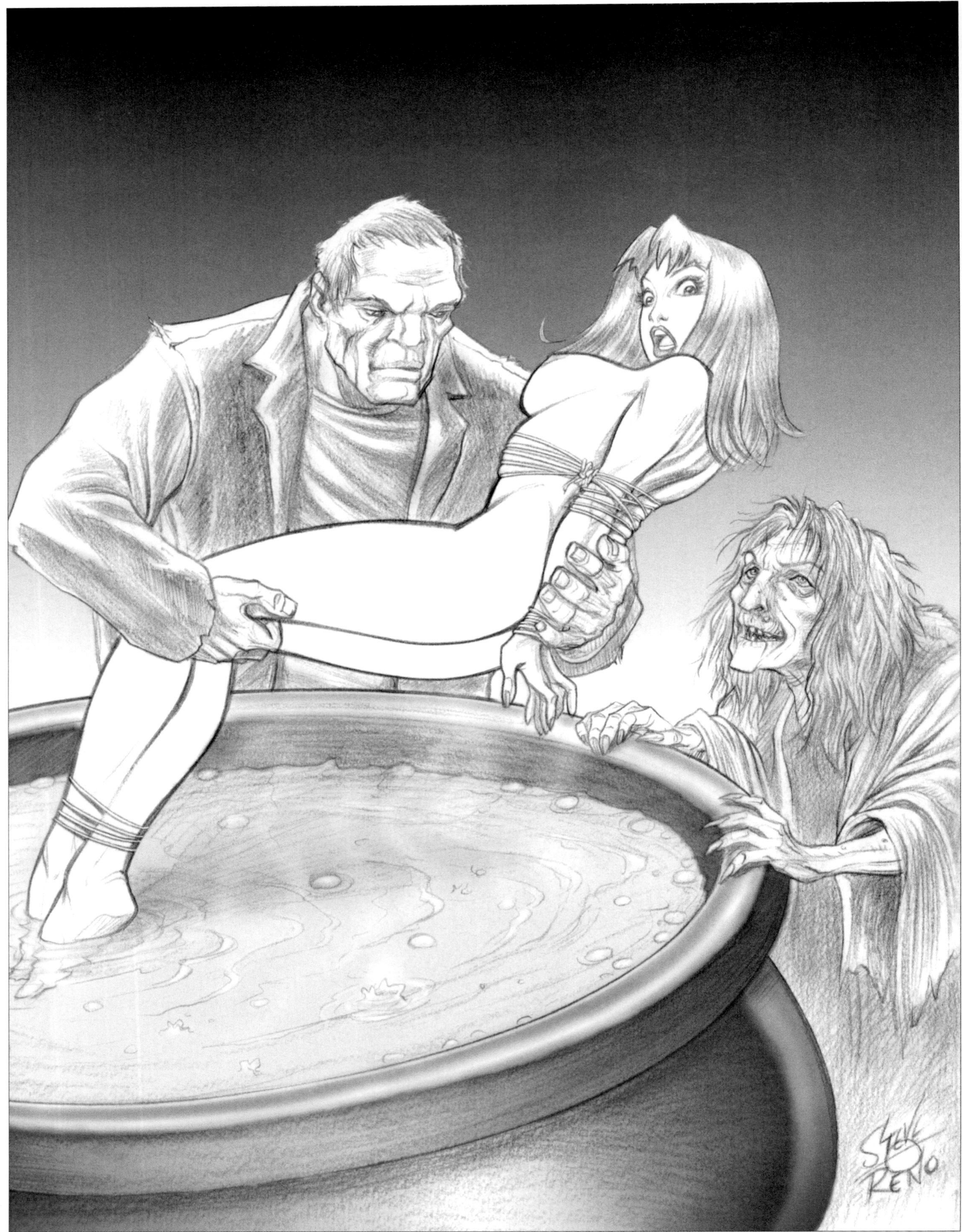

Witch's Brew

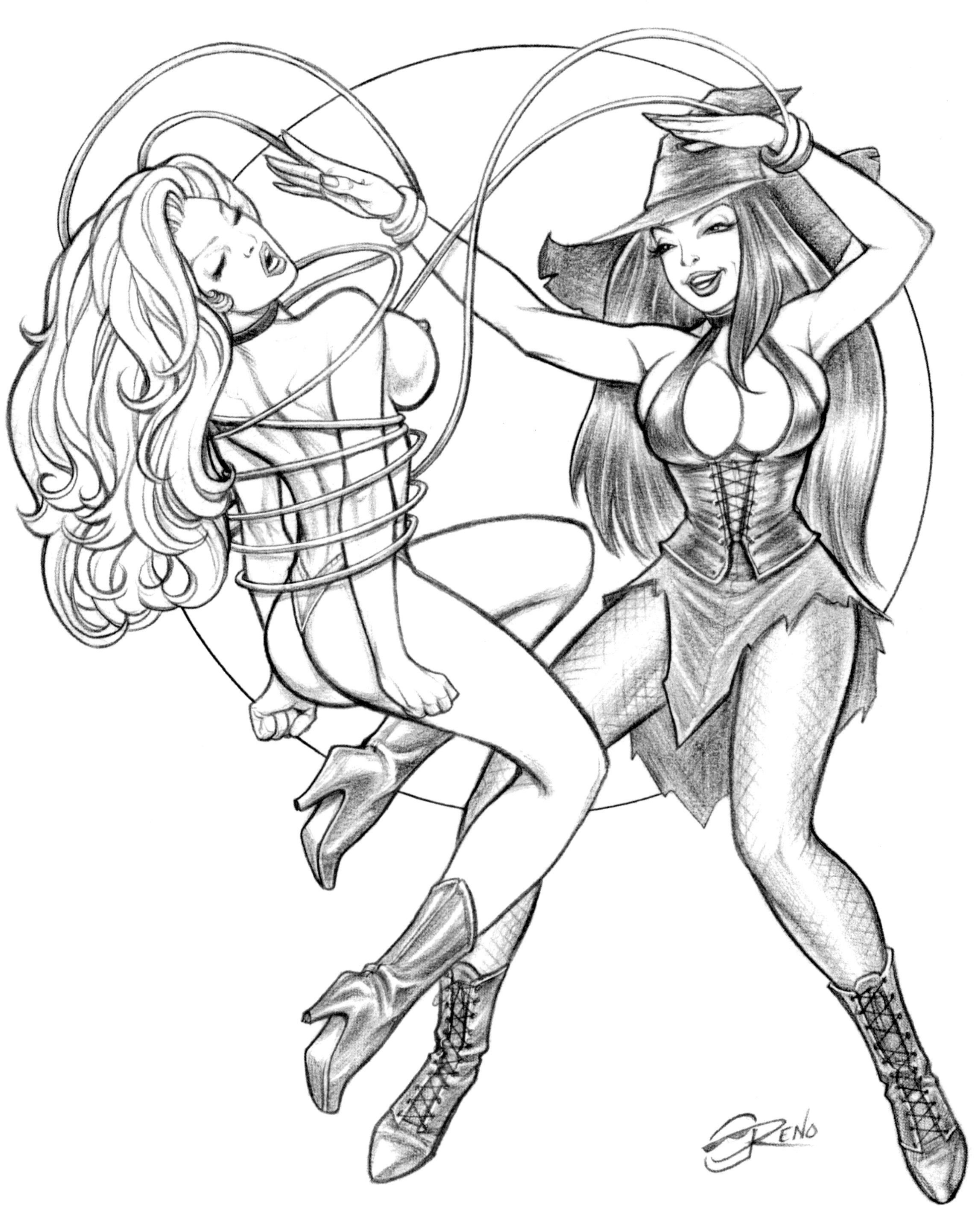

Coven Capture

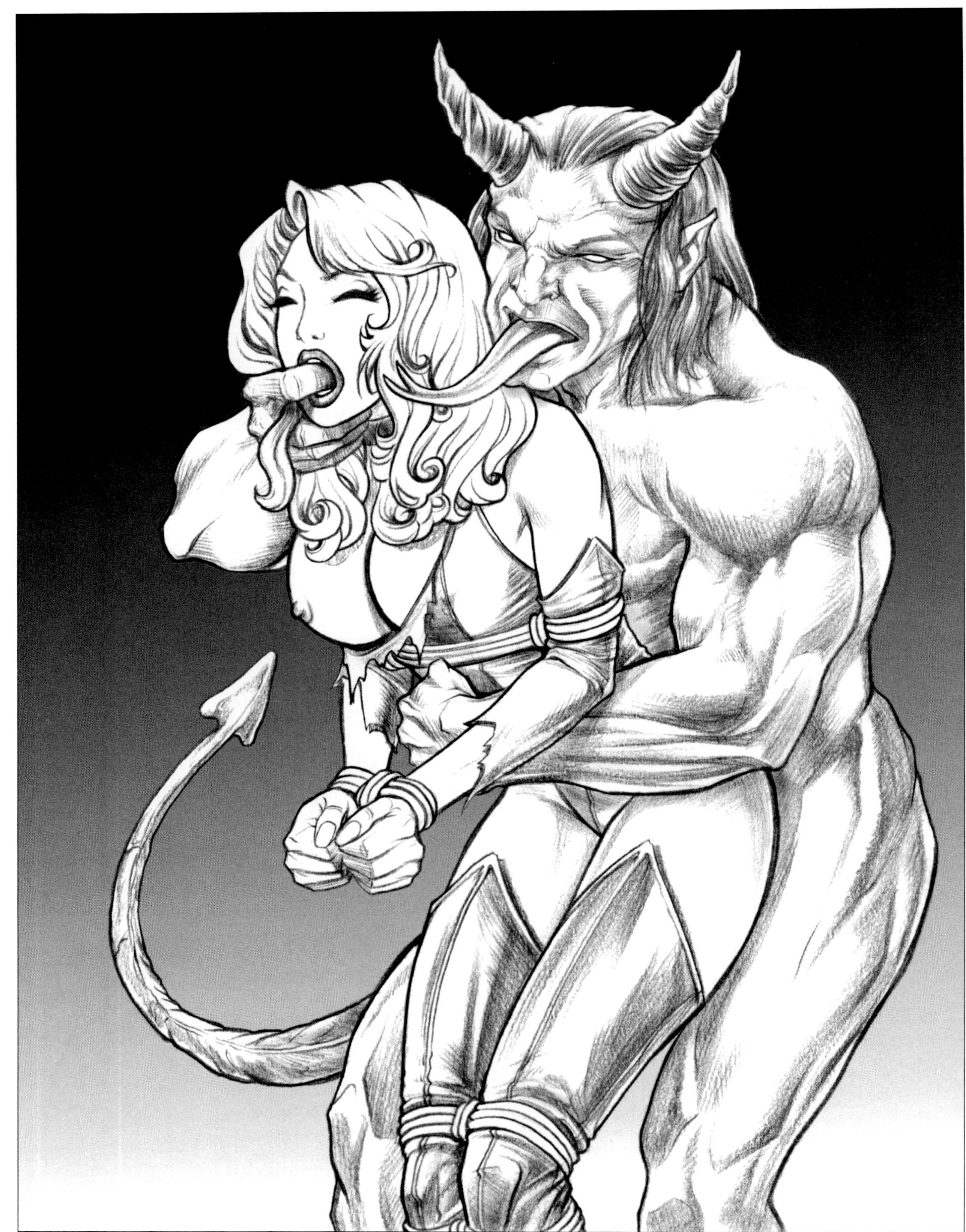

Morphistaphallus

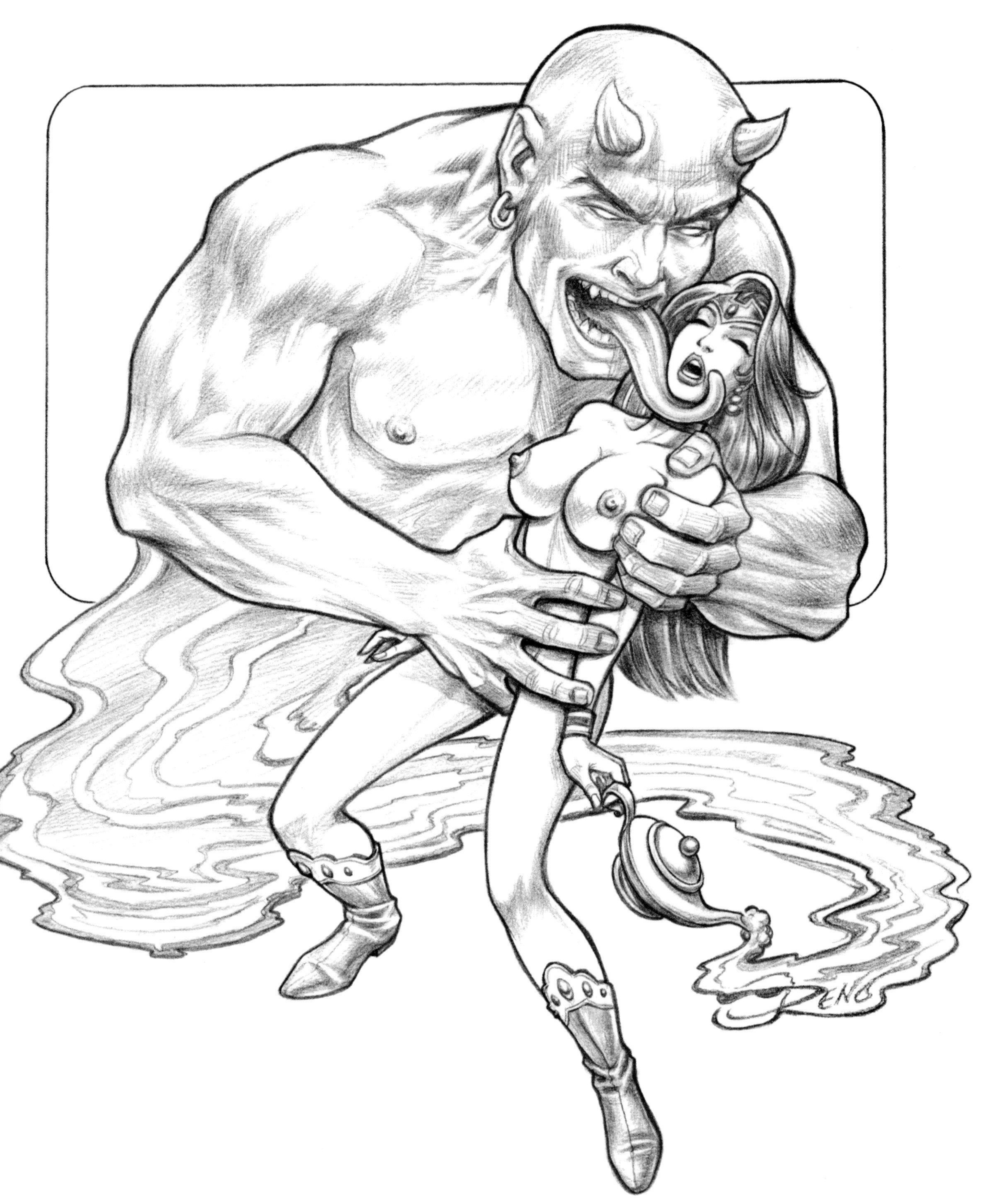

The Genie's Wish

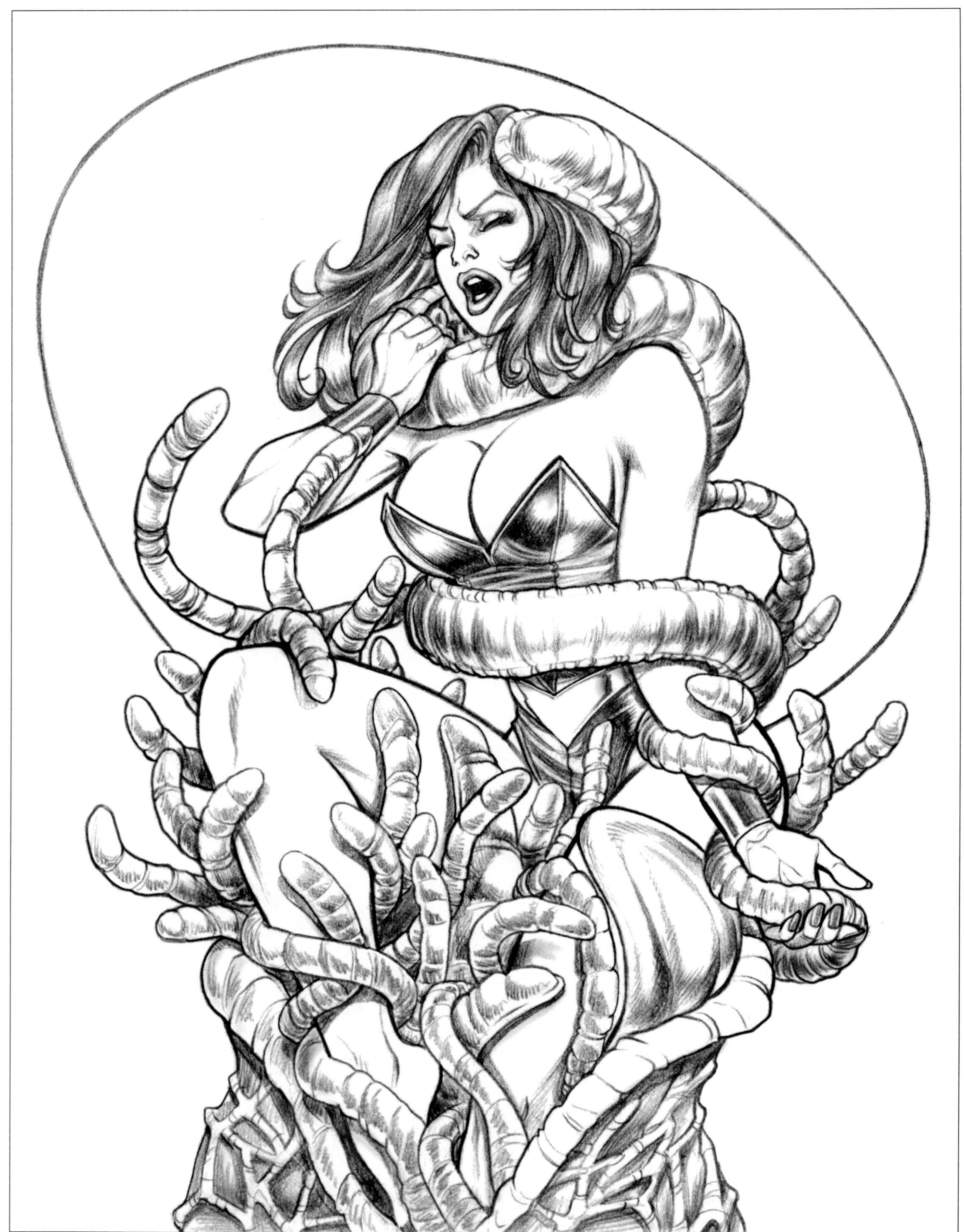

Tentacle Pod

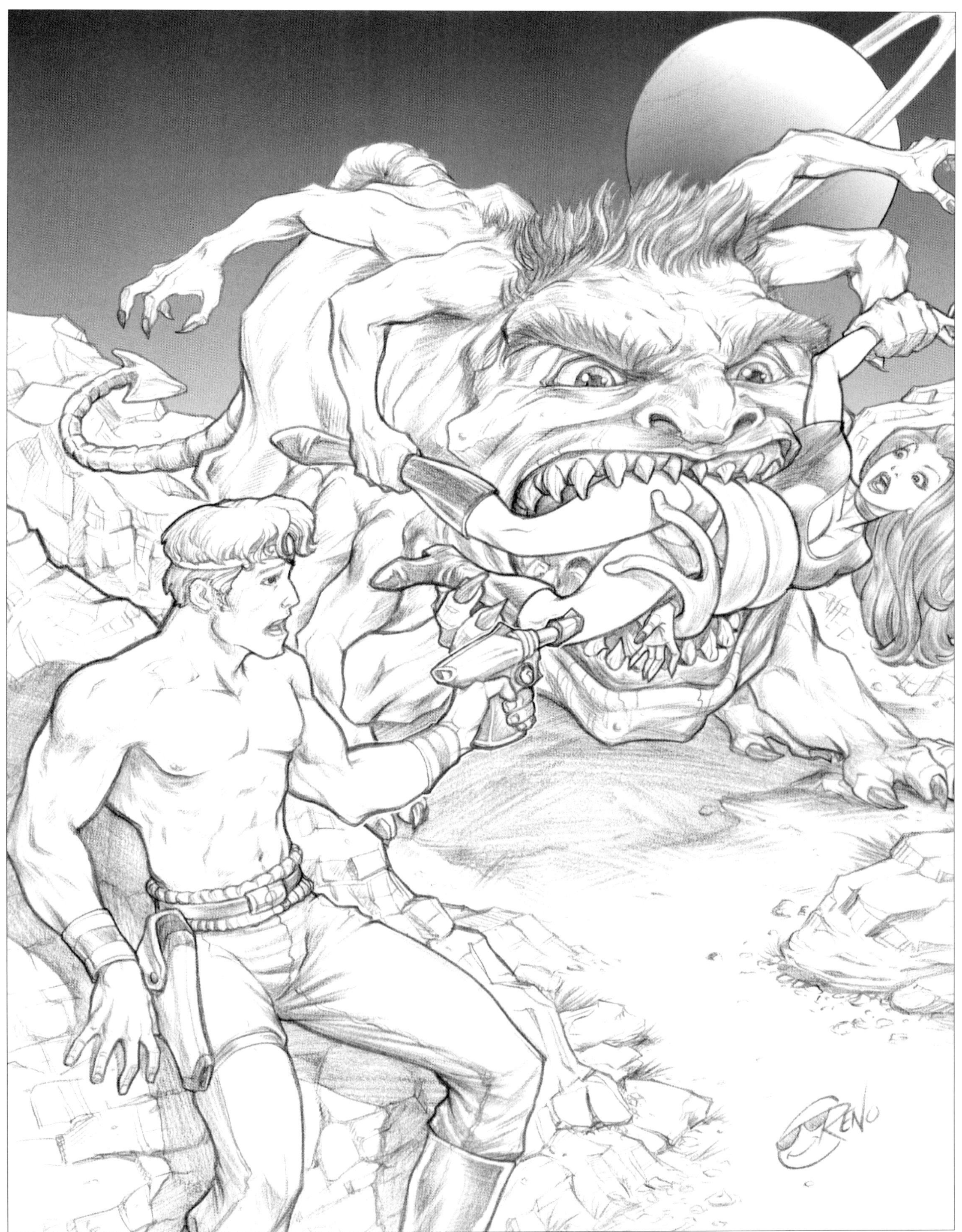

Flesh Gorgin'

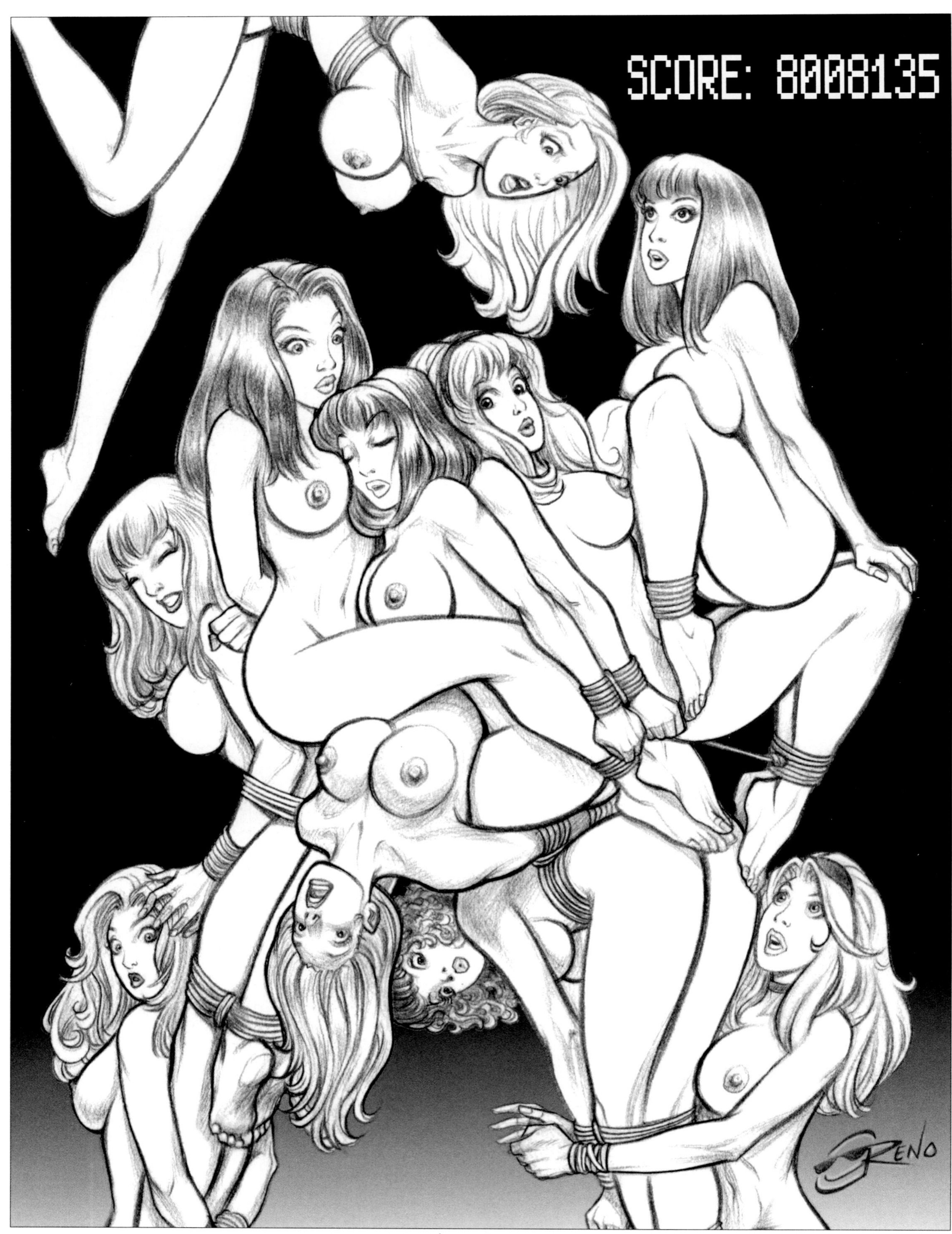

Playing Titres™

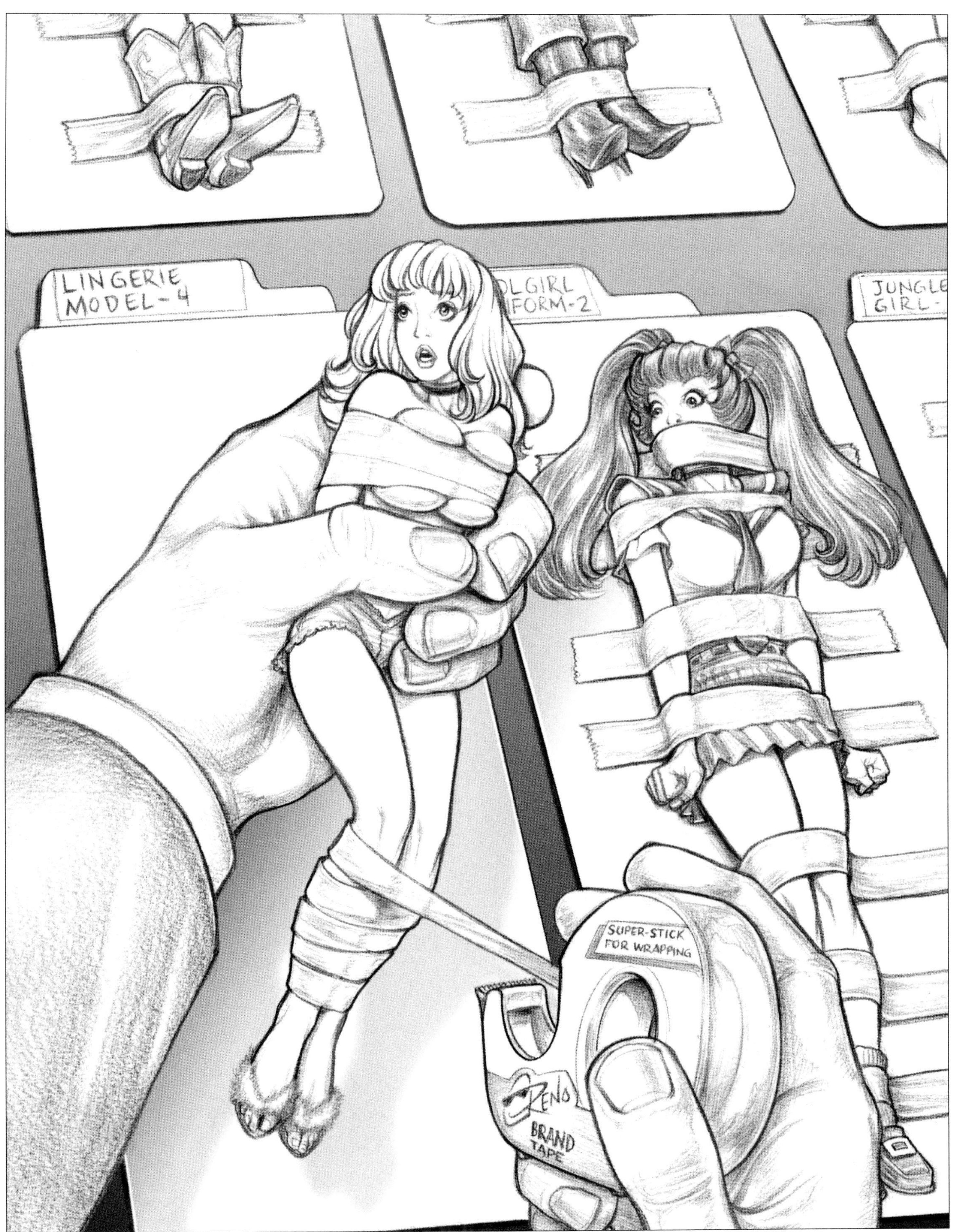

Collecting Figures

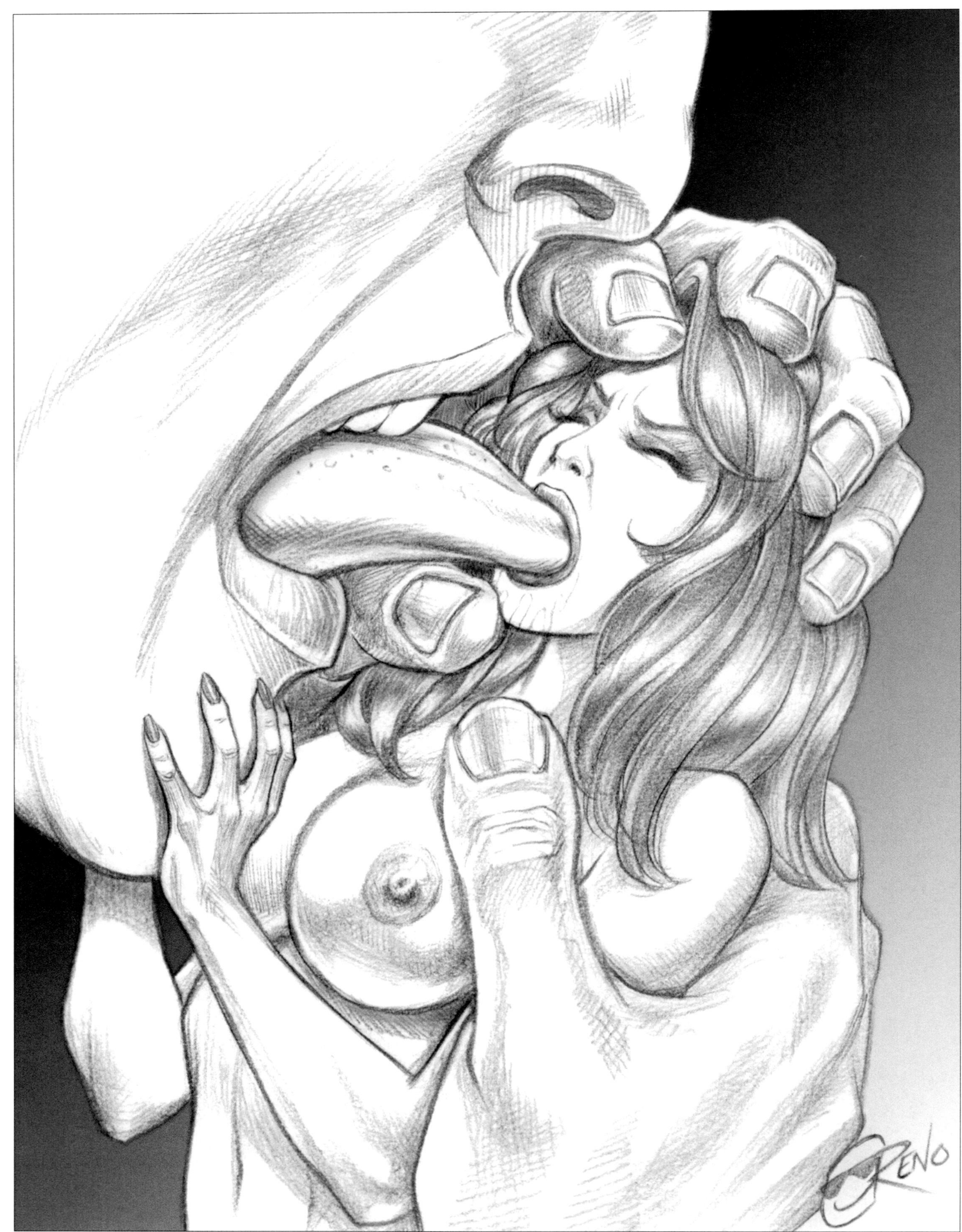

Giant Kiss

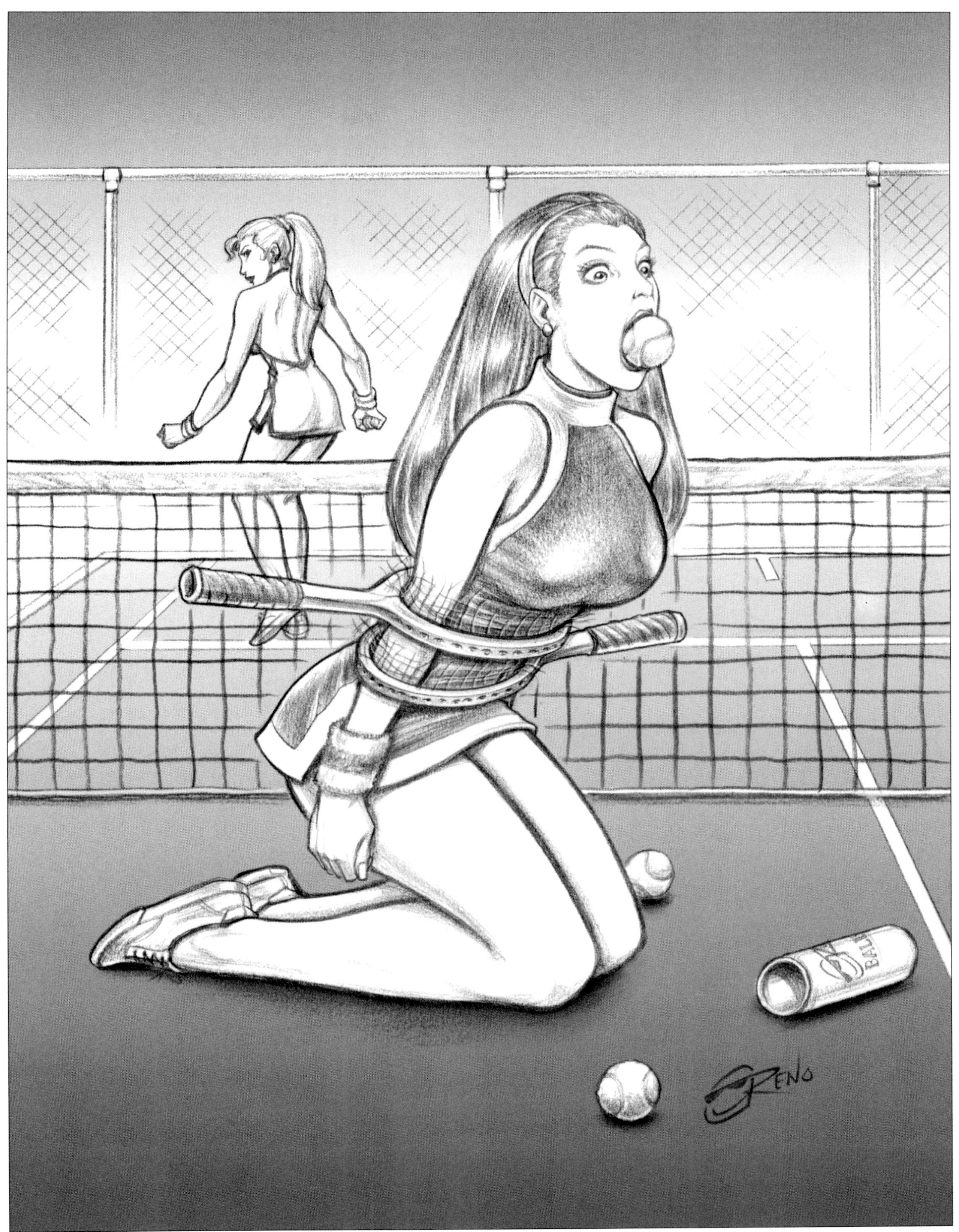

Game, Set, Match!

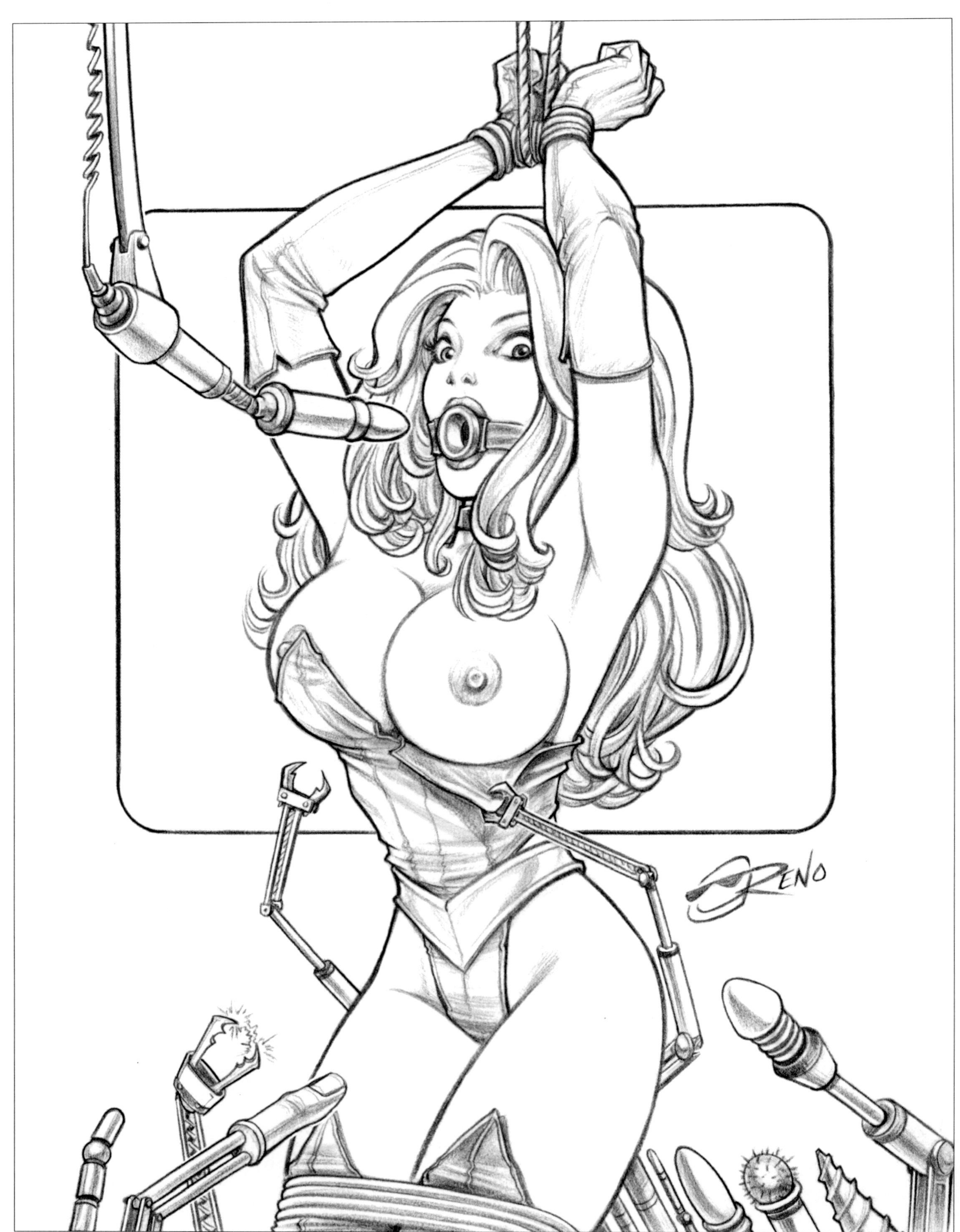

Steve-O-Reno's Vibe-O-Rama

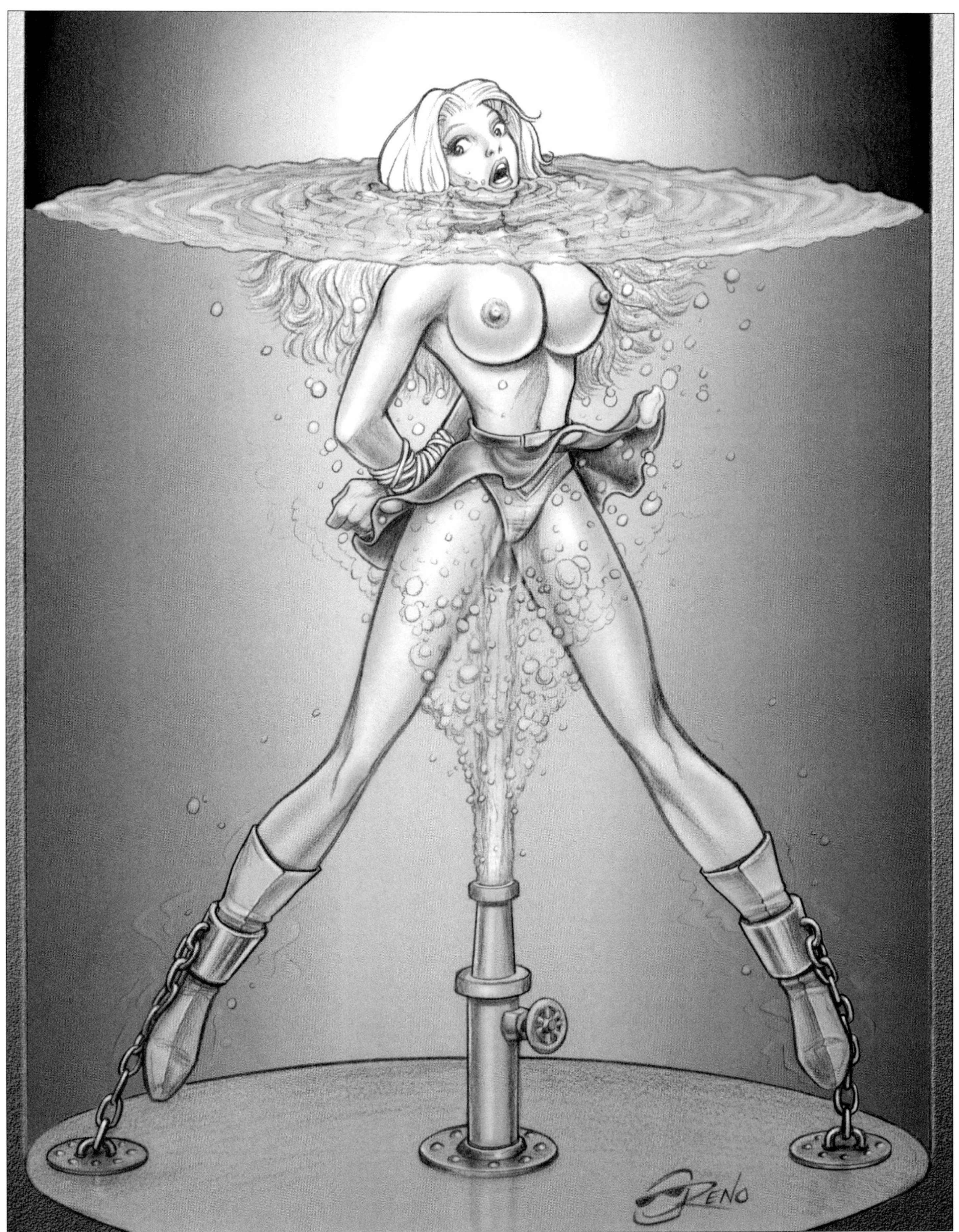

Mixed Feelings

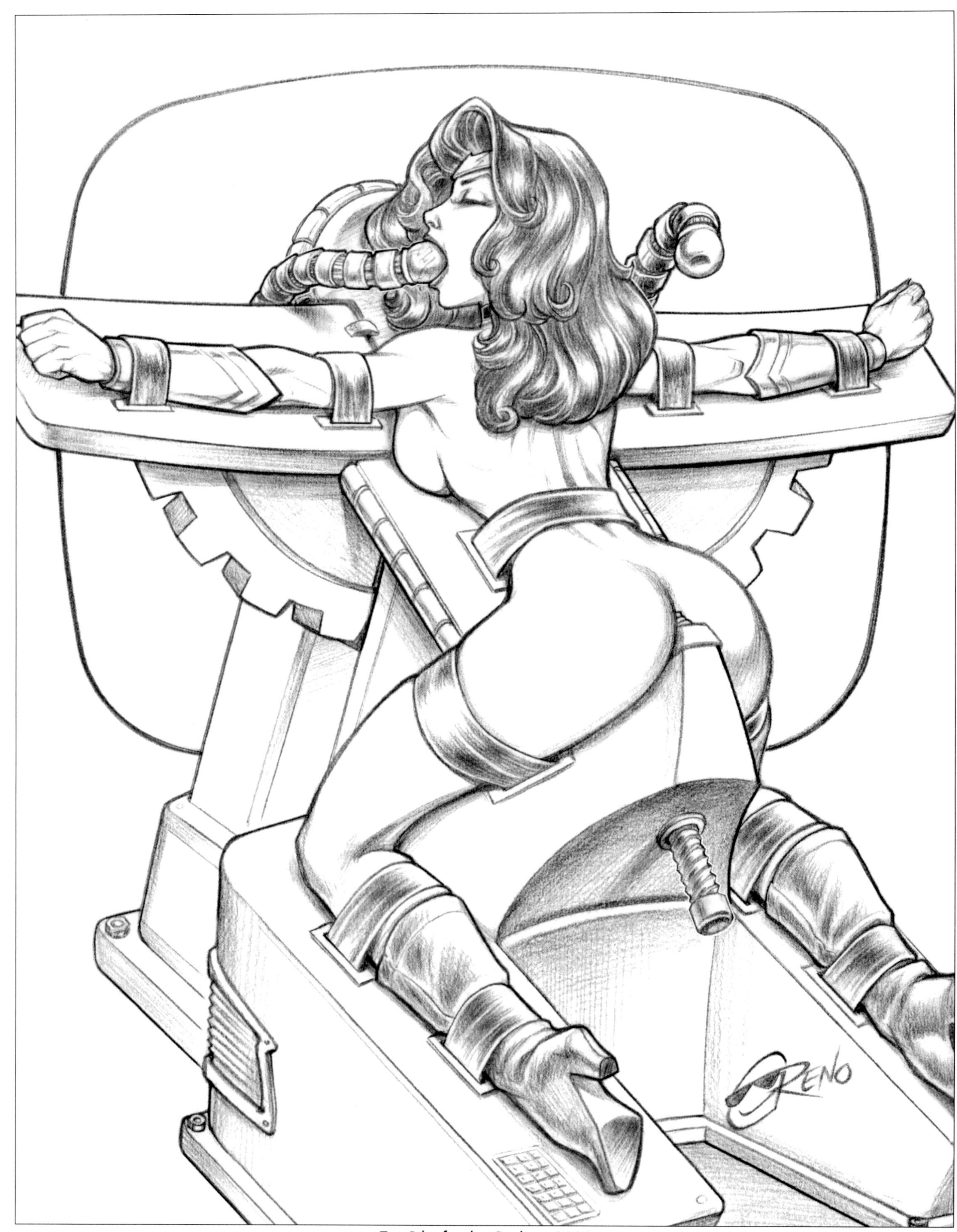

Test Pilot for the Oralizer 3000

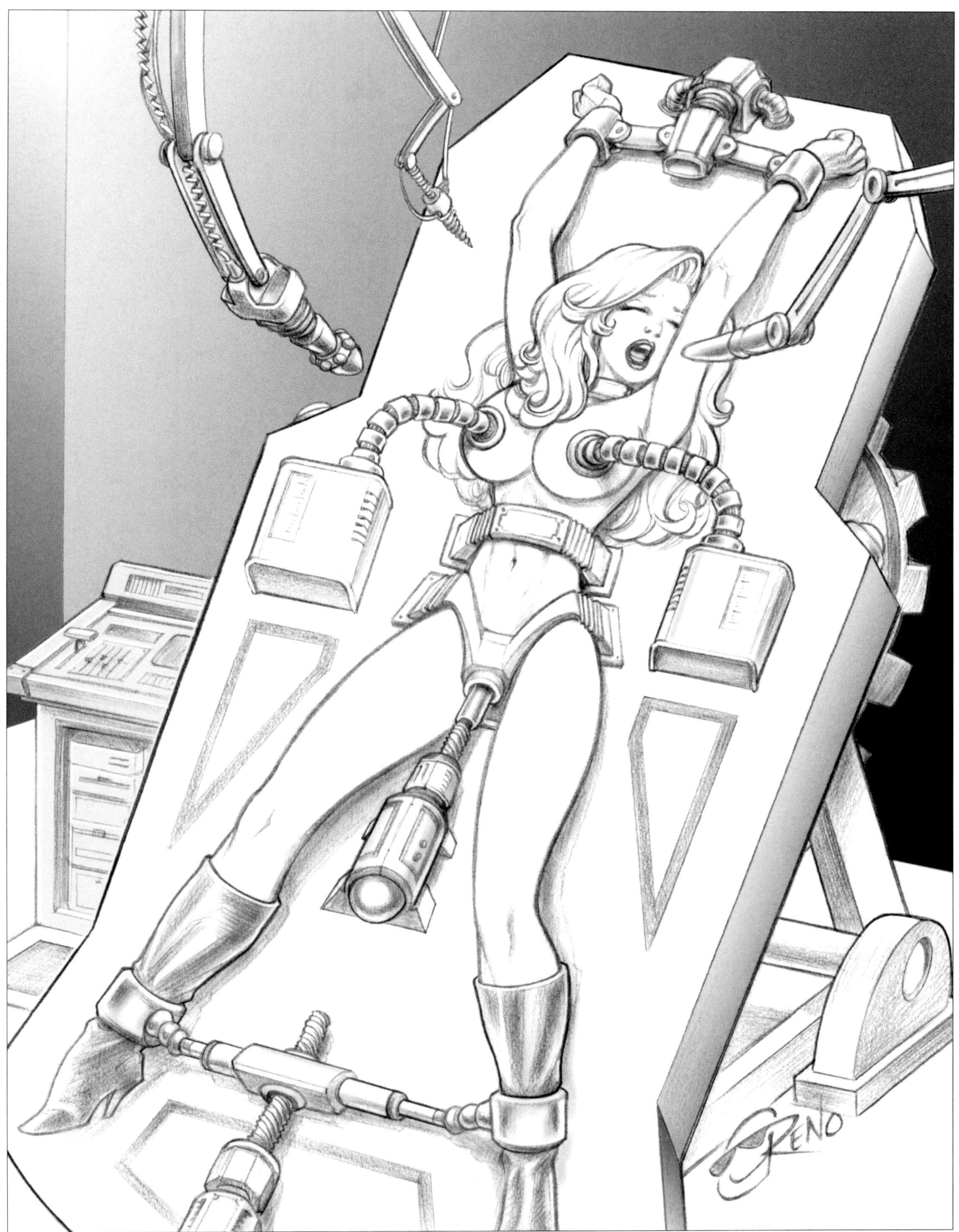

Sexperiment

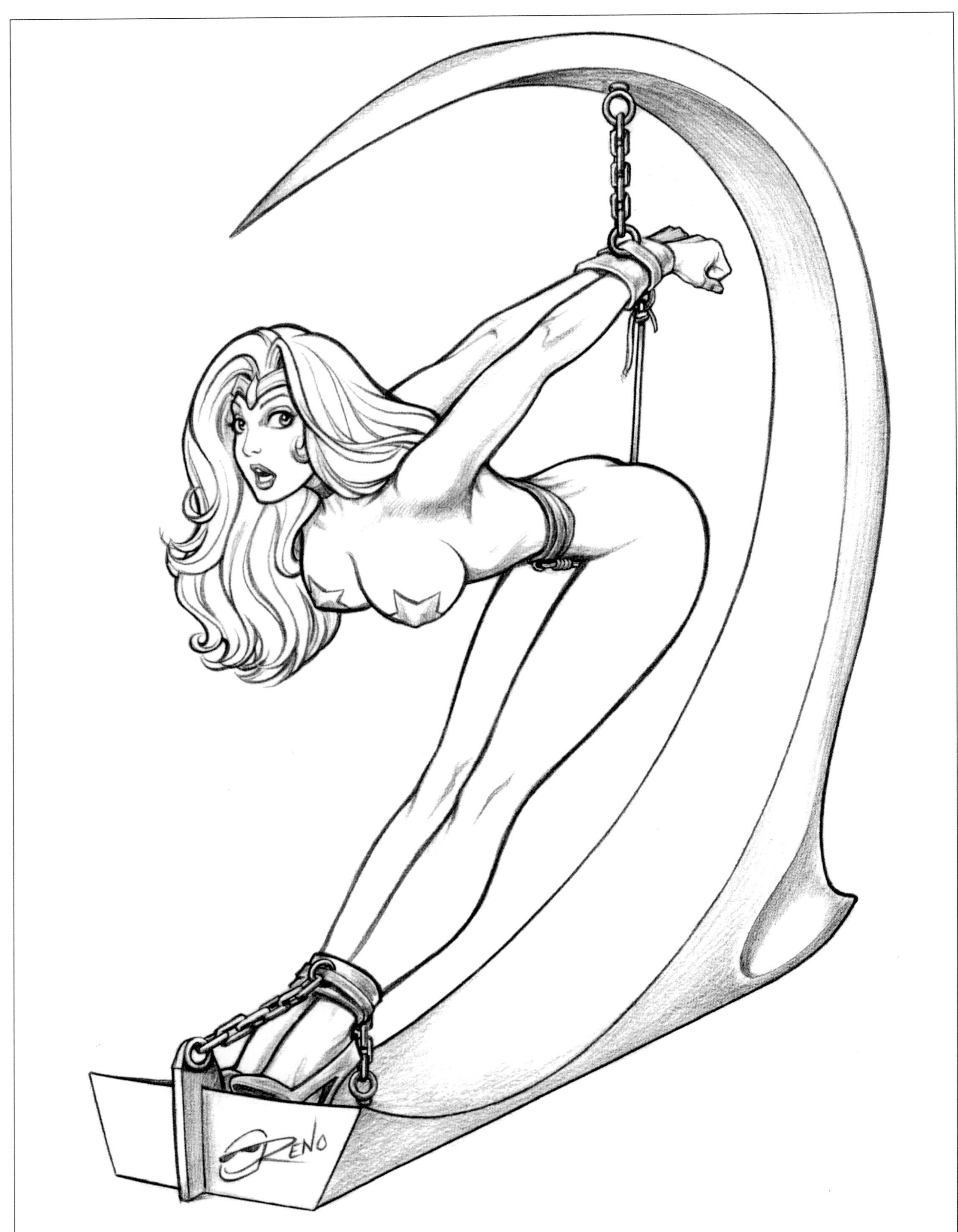

Celestial

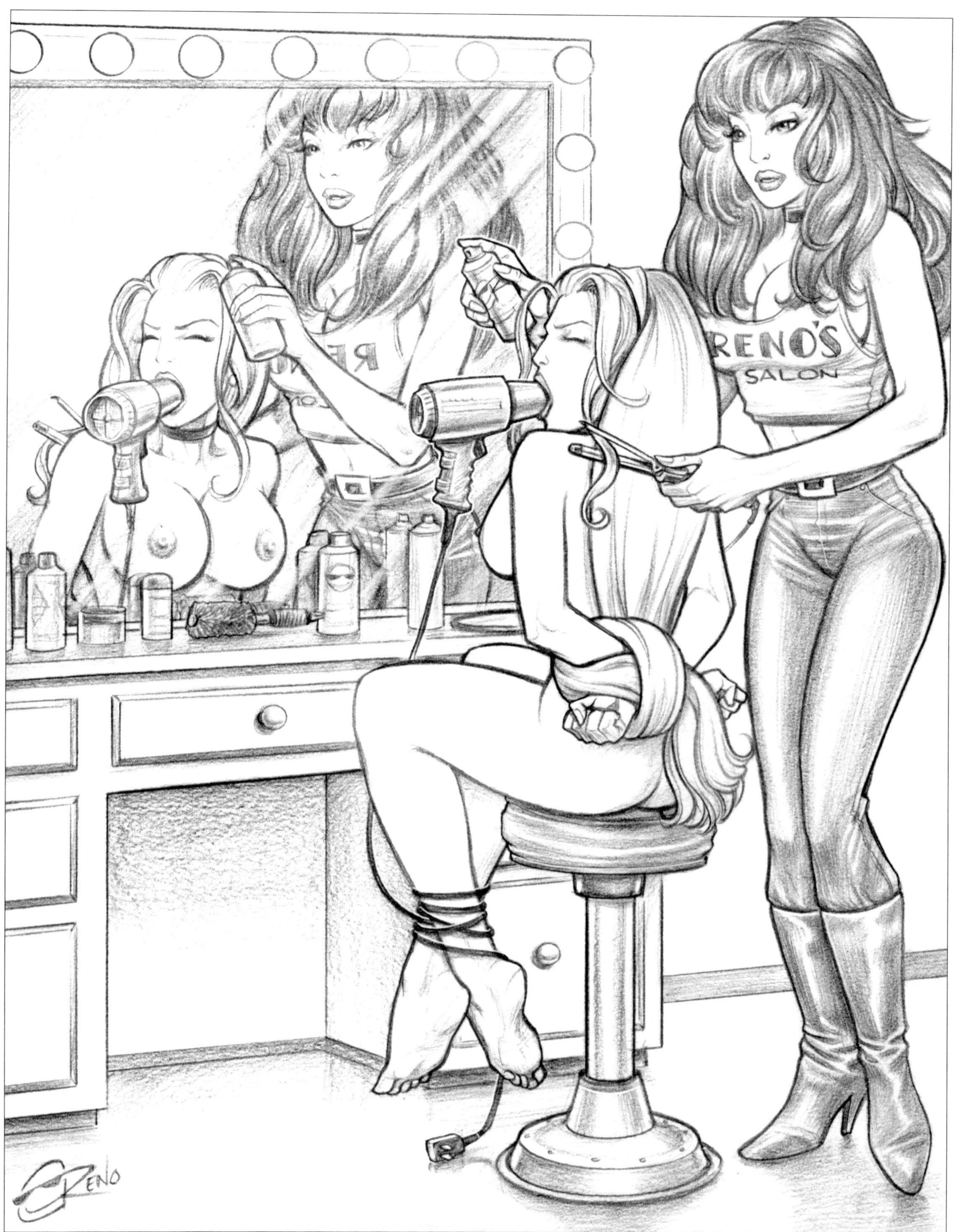

It's A Blow Job

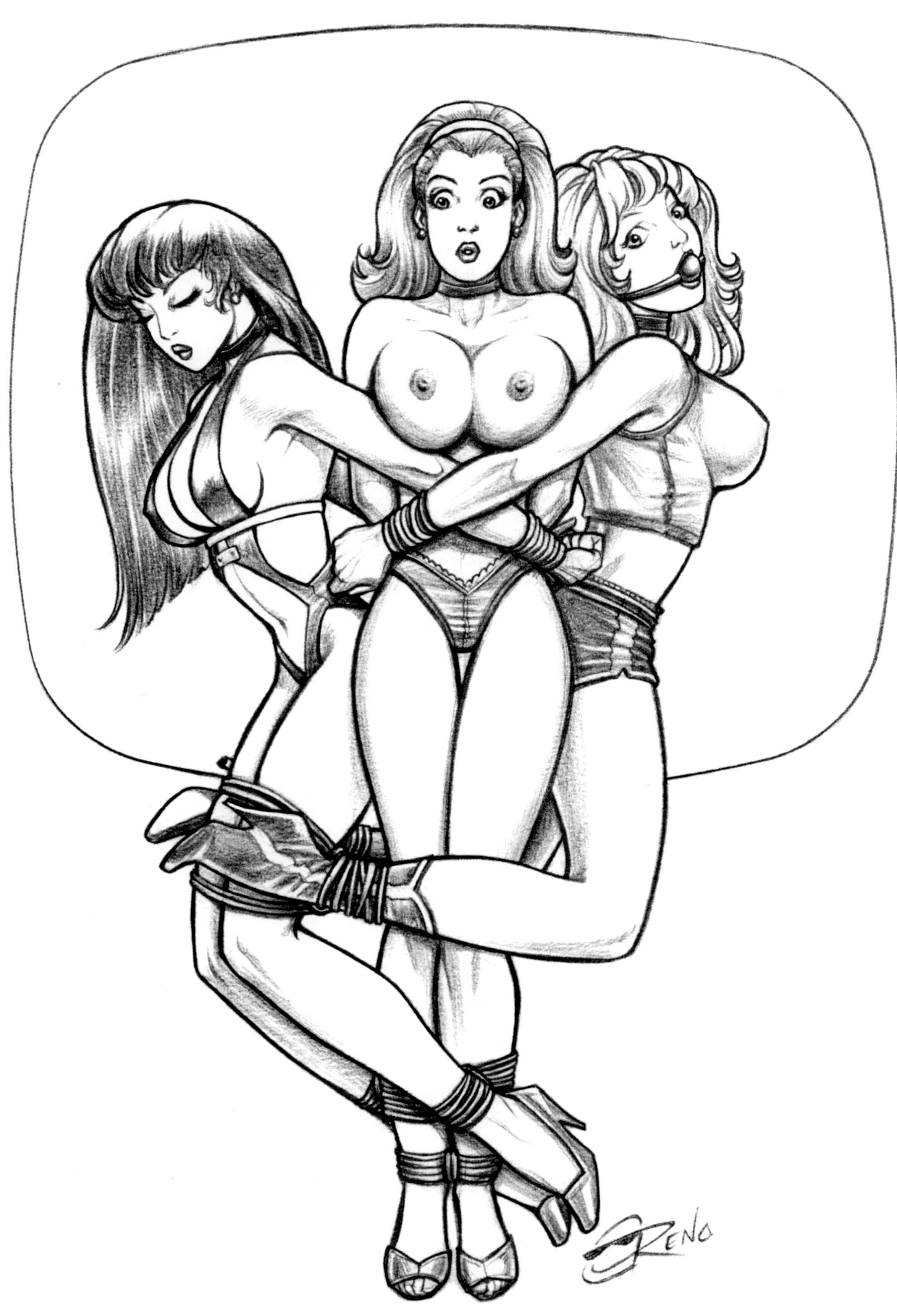

Bound by Desire

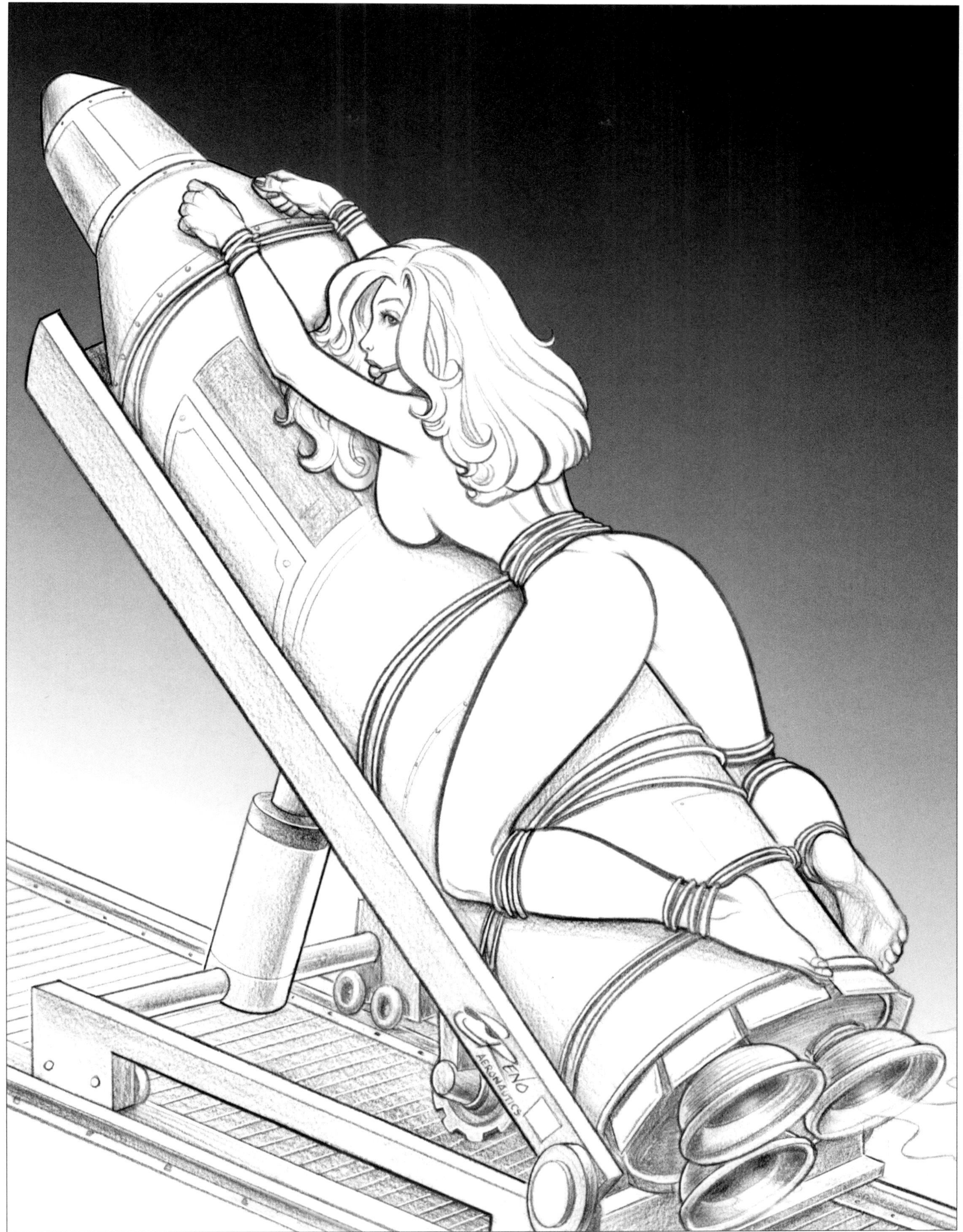

Miss "L"

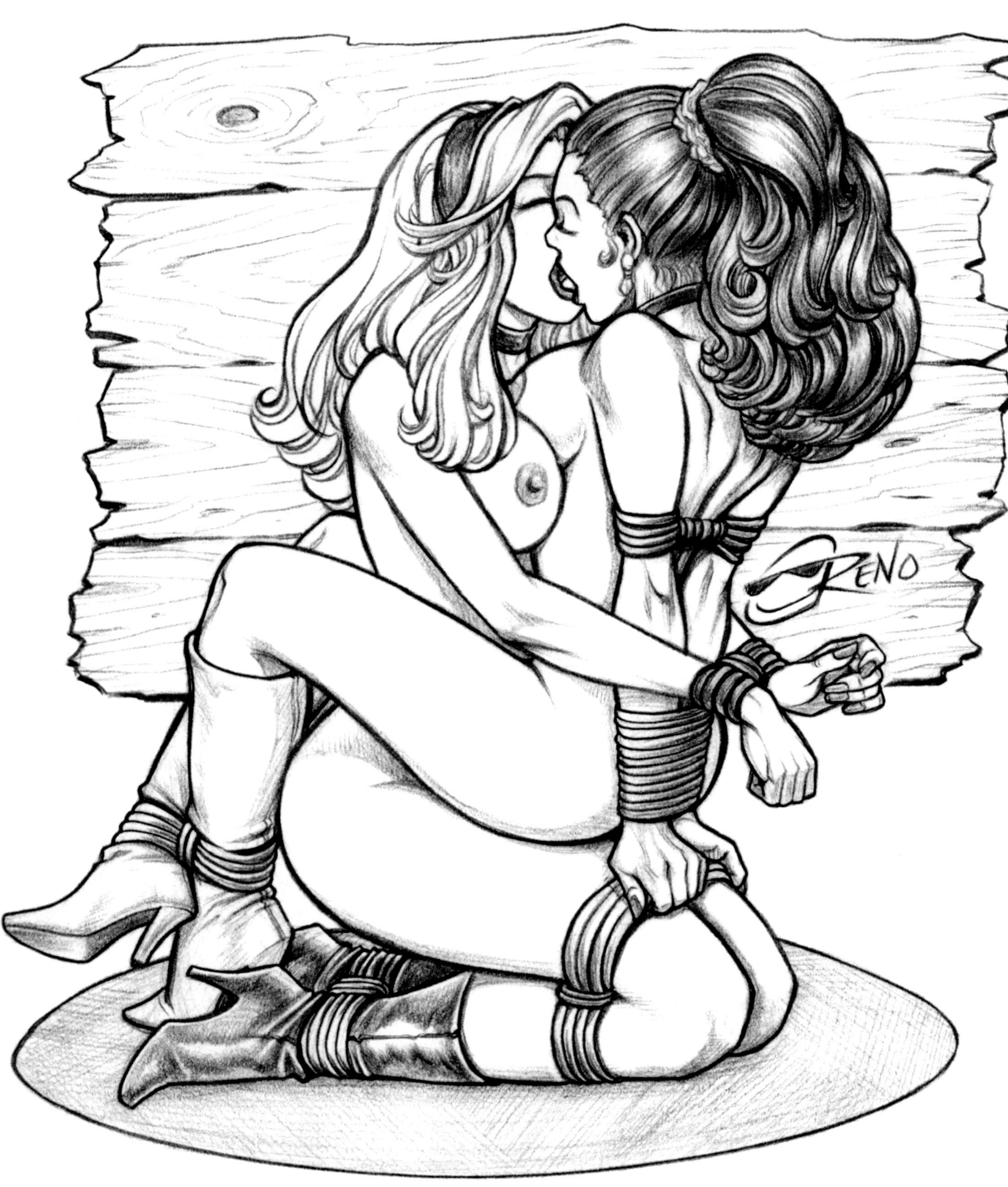

Tongue Wrasslin'

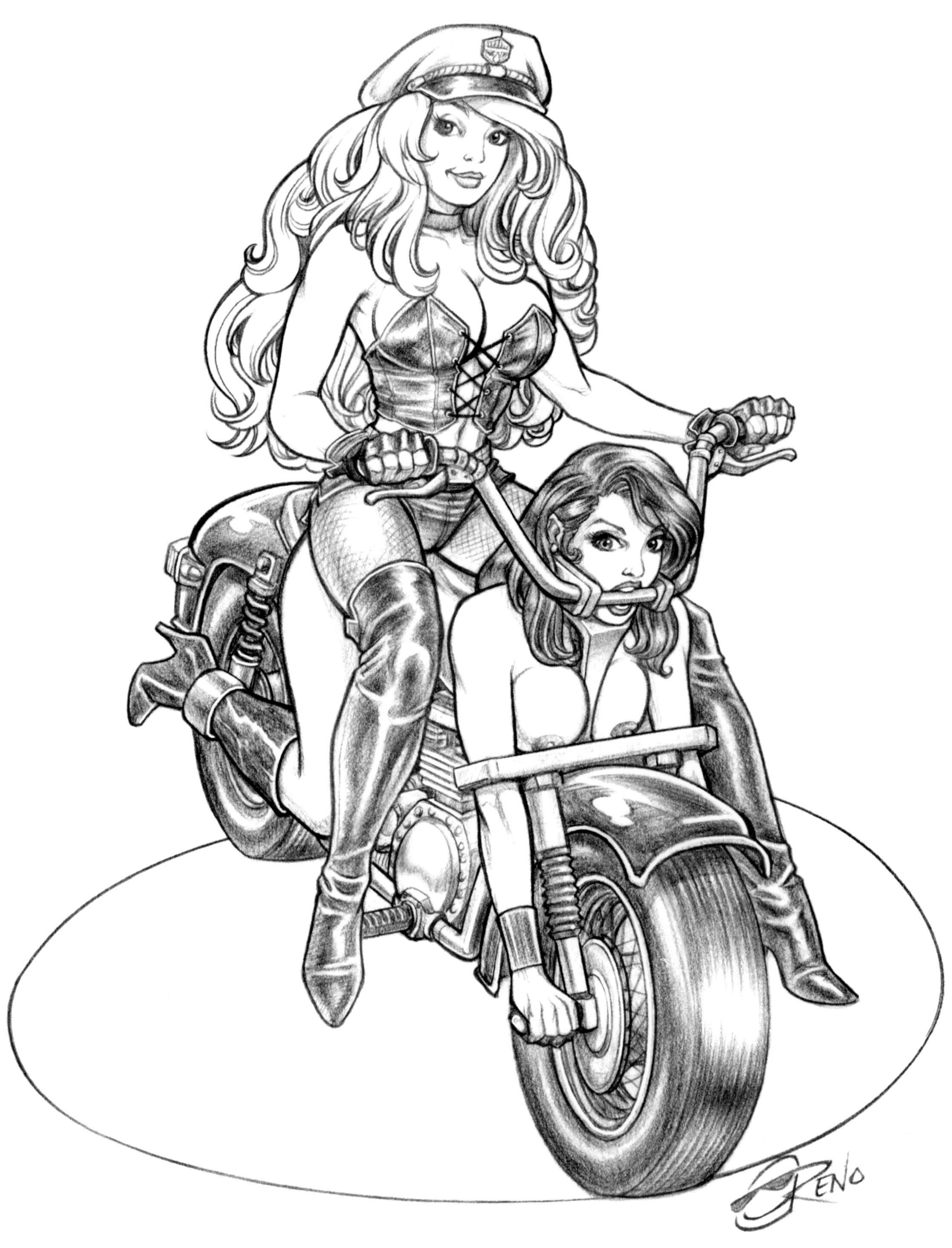

Biker Chick and Chicker Bike

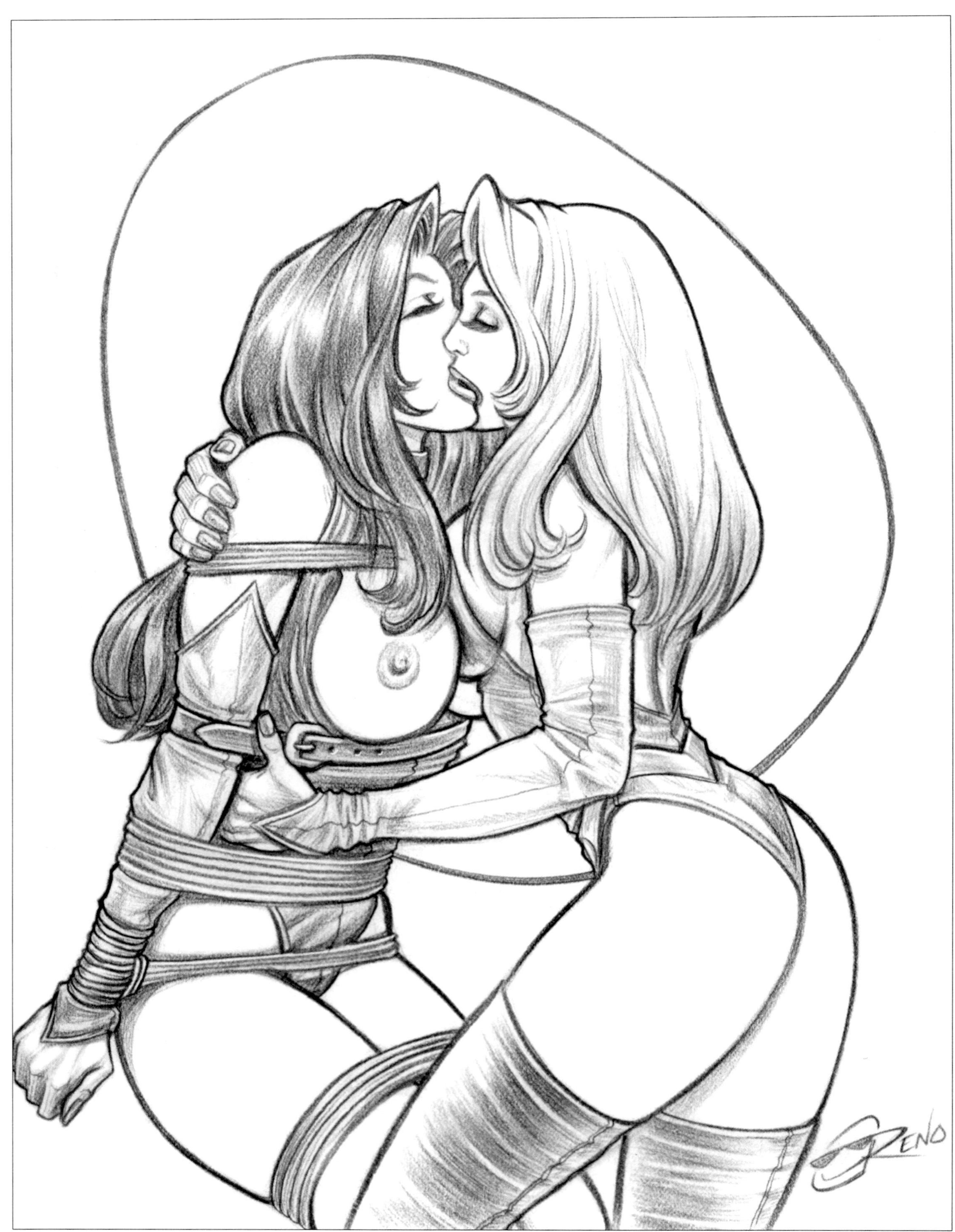

Female Bonding

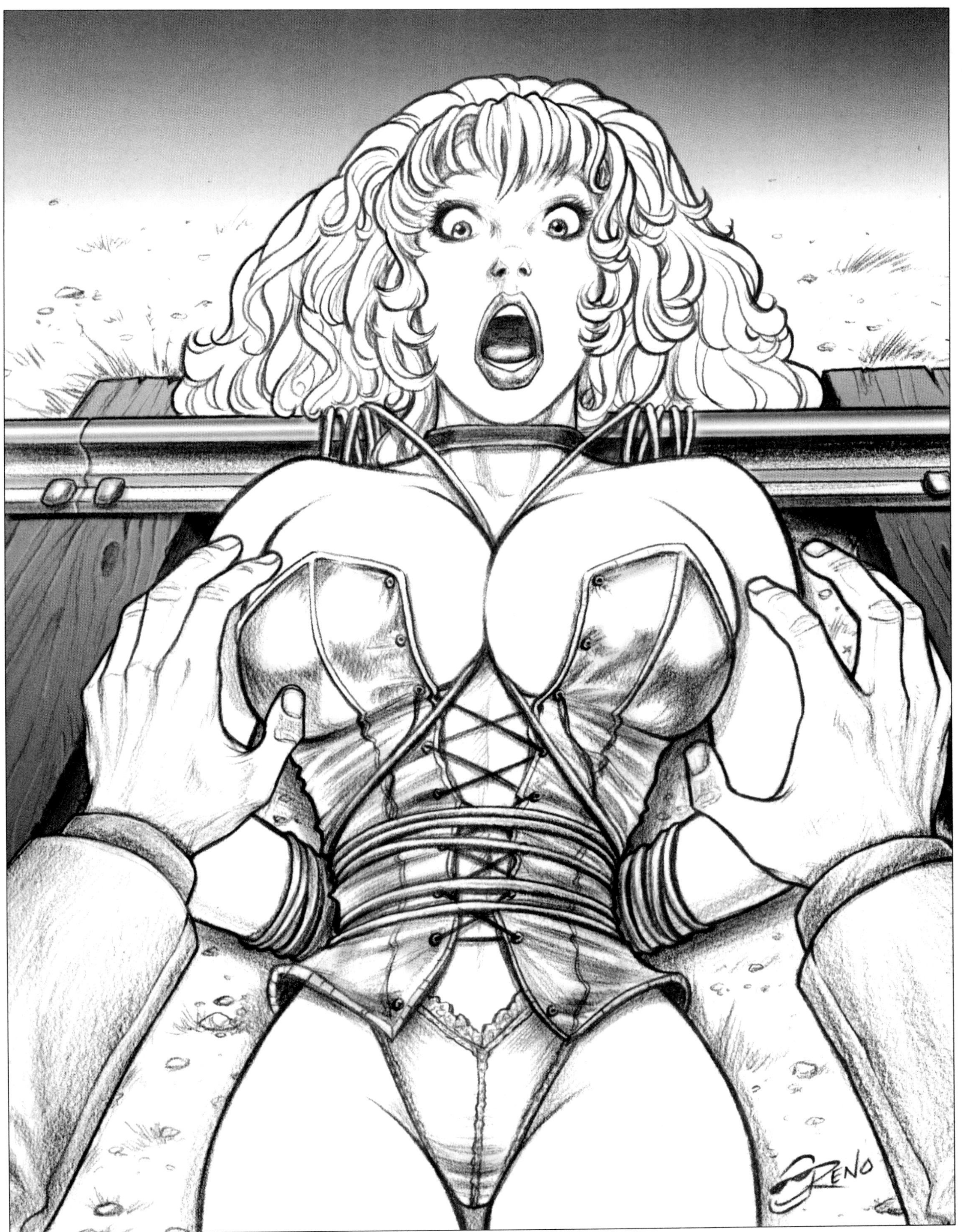

Side Tracked

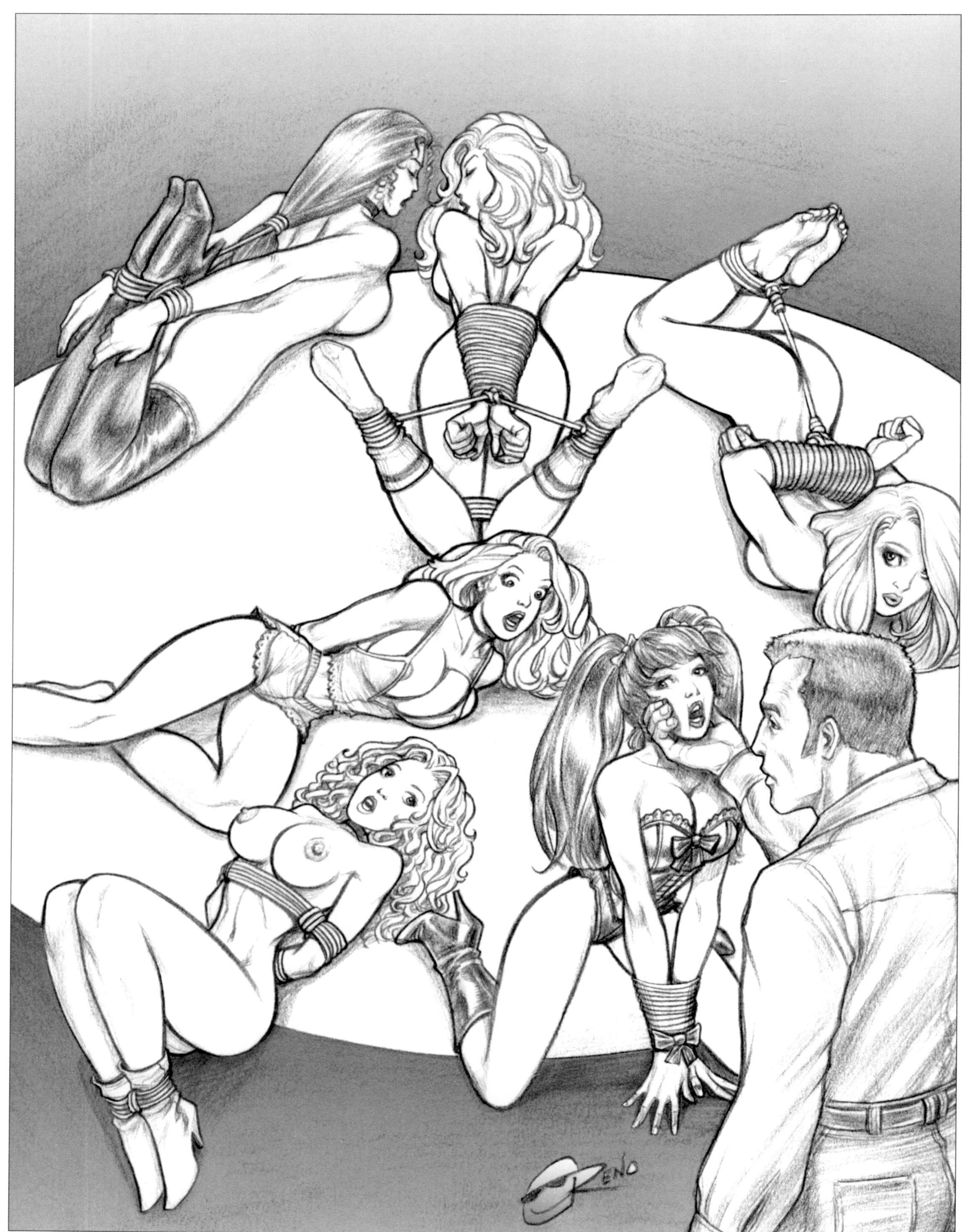

Floor Models

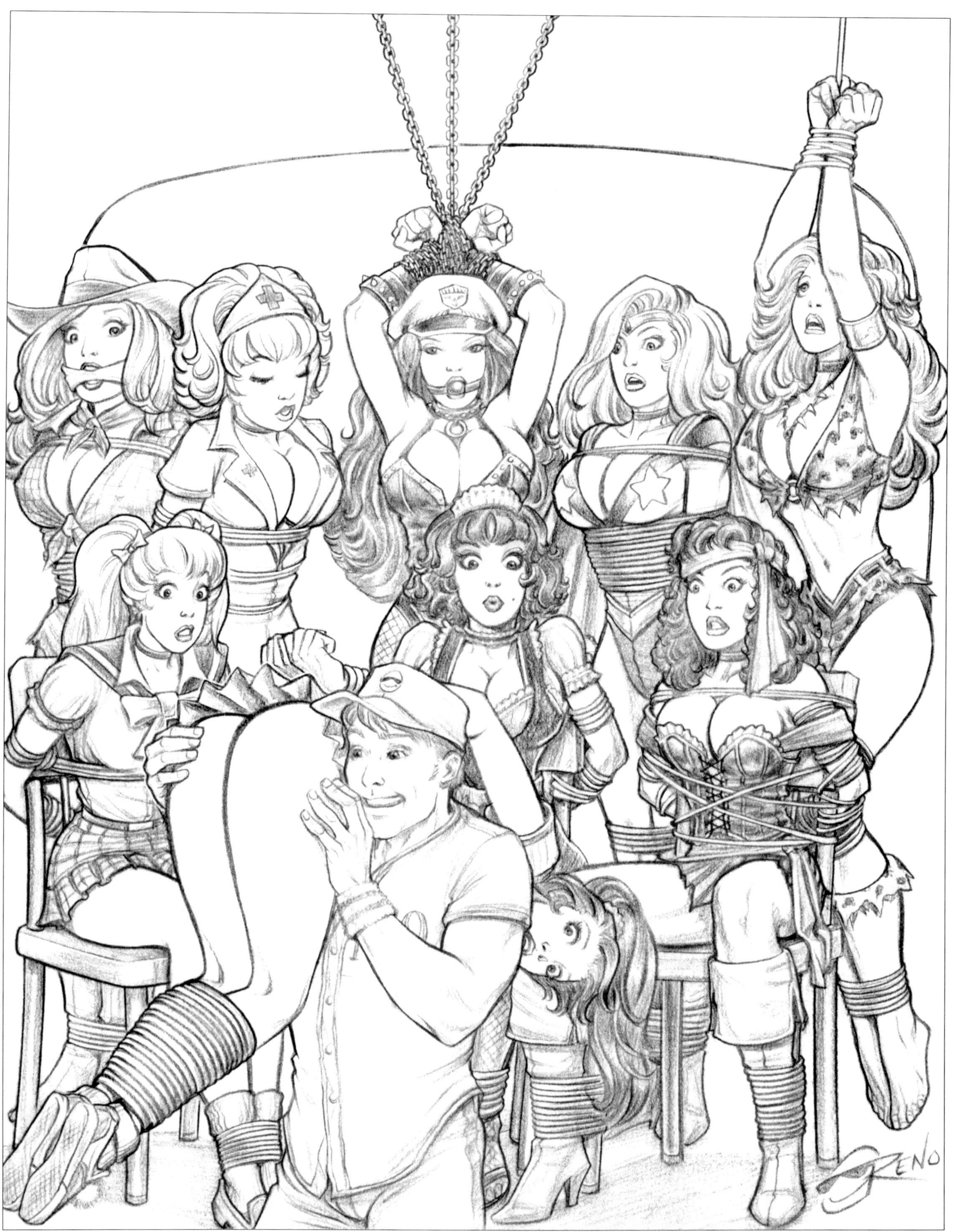

Fantasy League

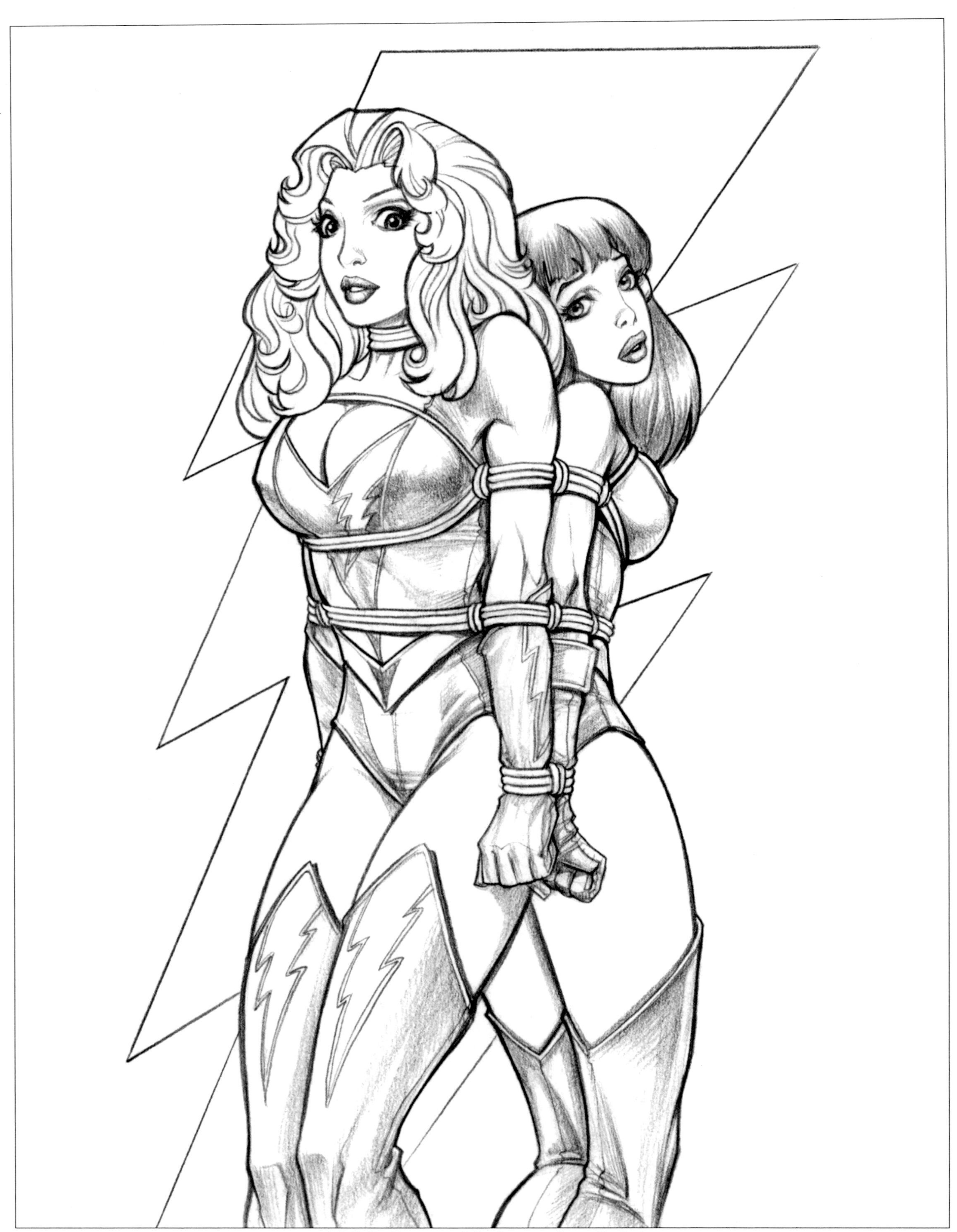

AC/DC - Captives of the Perverse Reno-Gades!

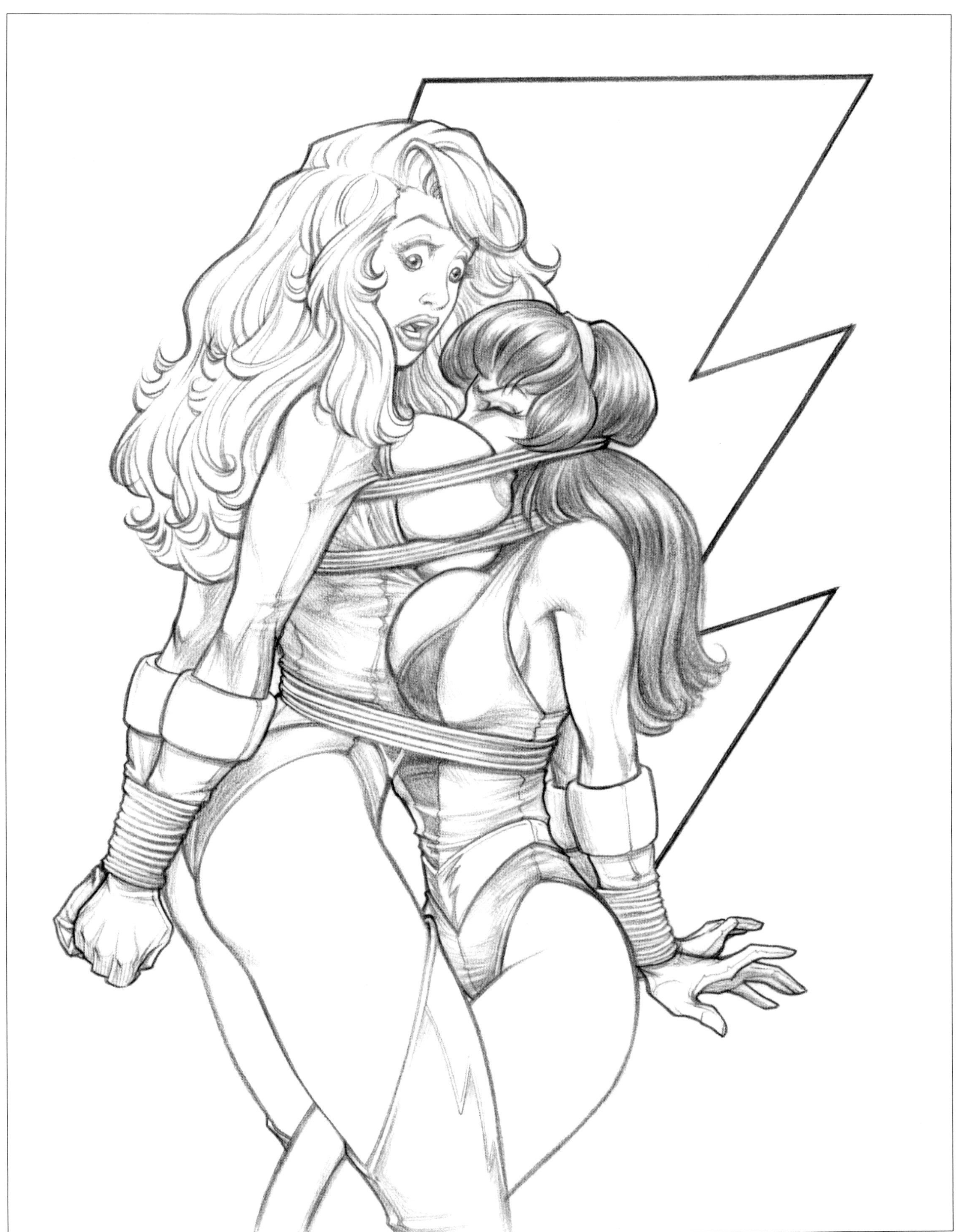

Escape Proves Problematic

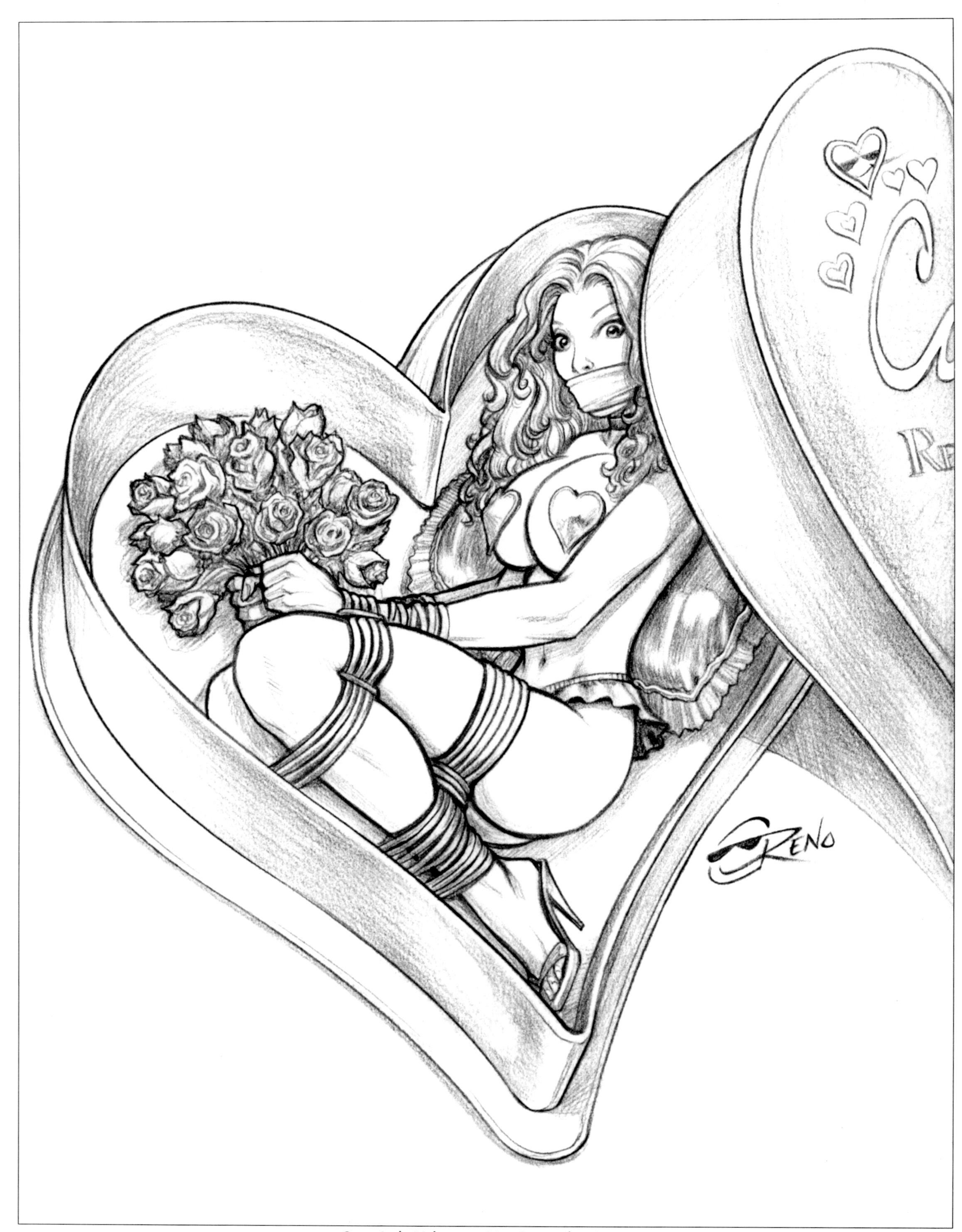

Stay, Little Valentine. No, Seriously - STAY!

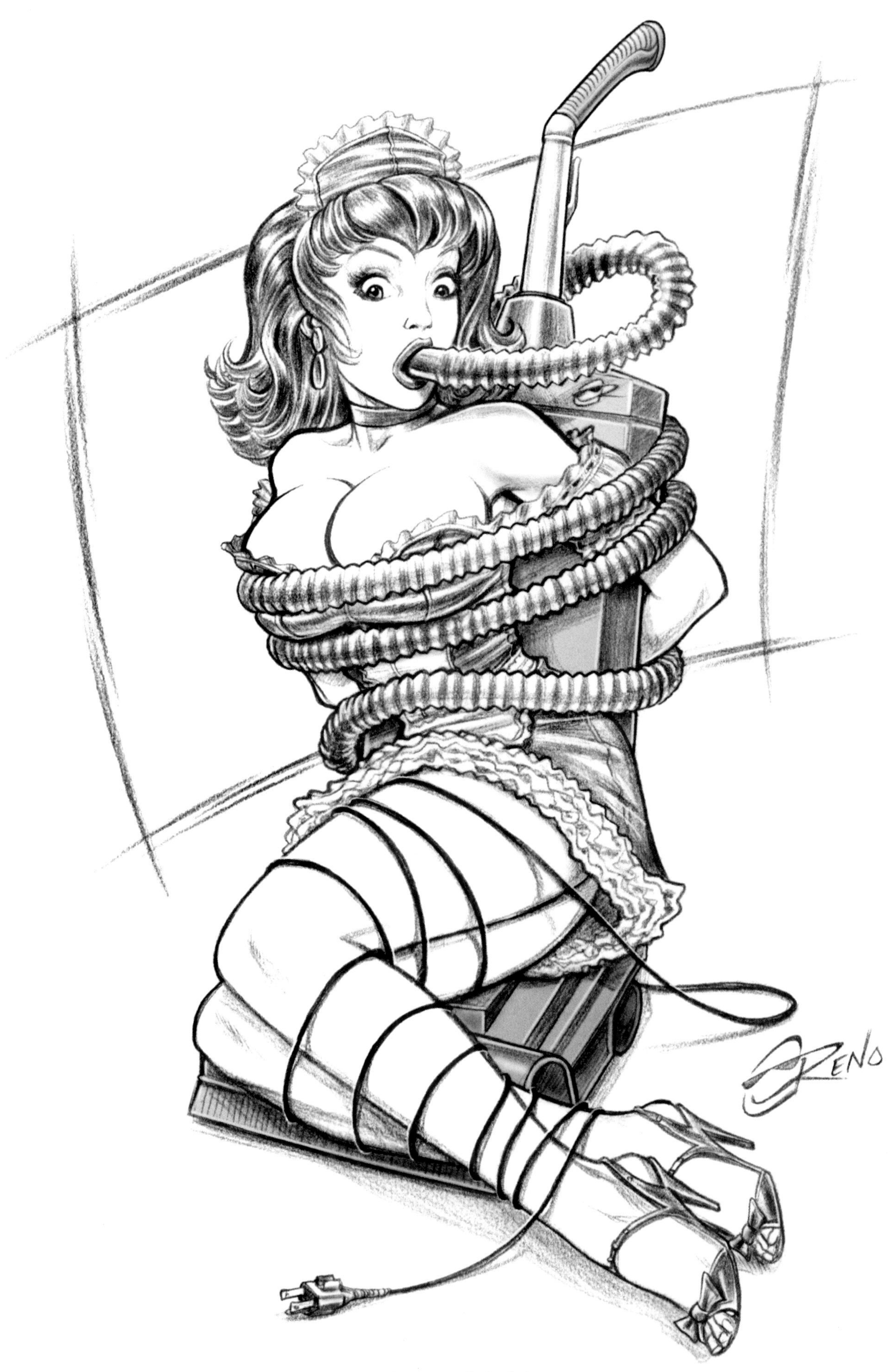

Housework Sucks!

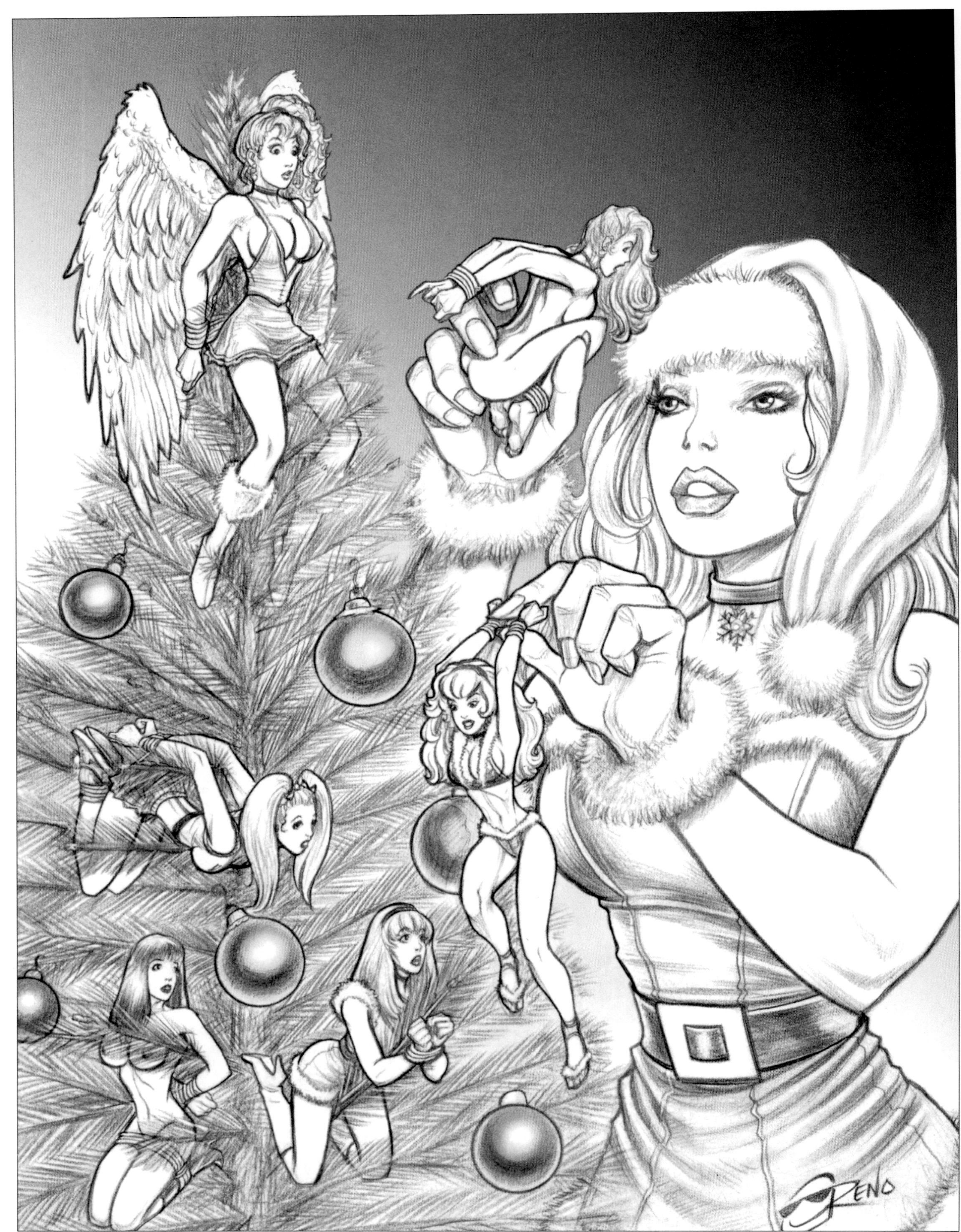

Tormented Ornaments

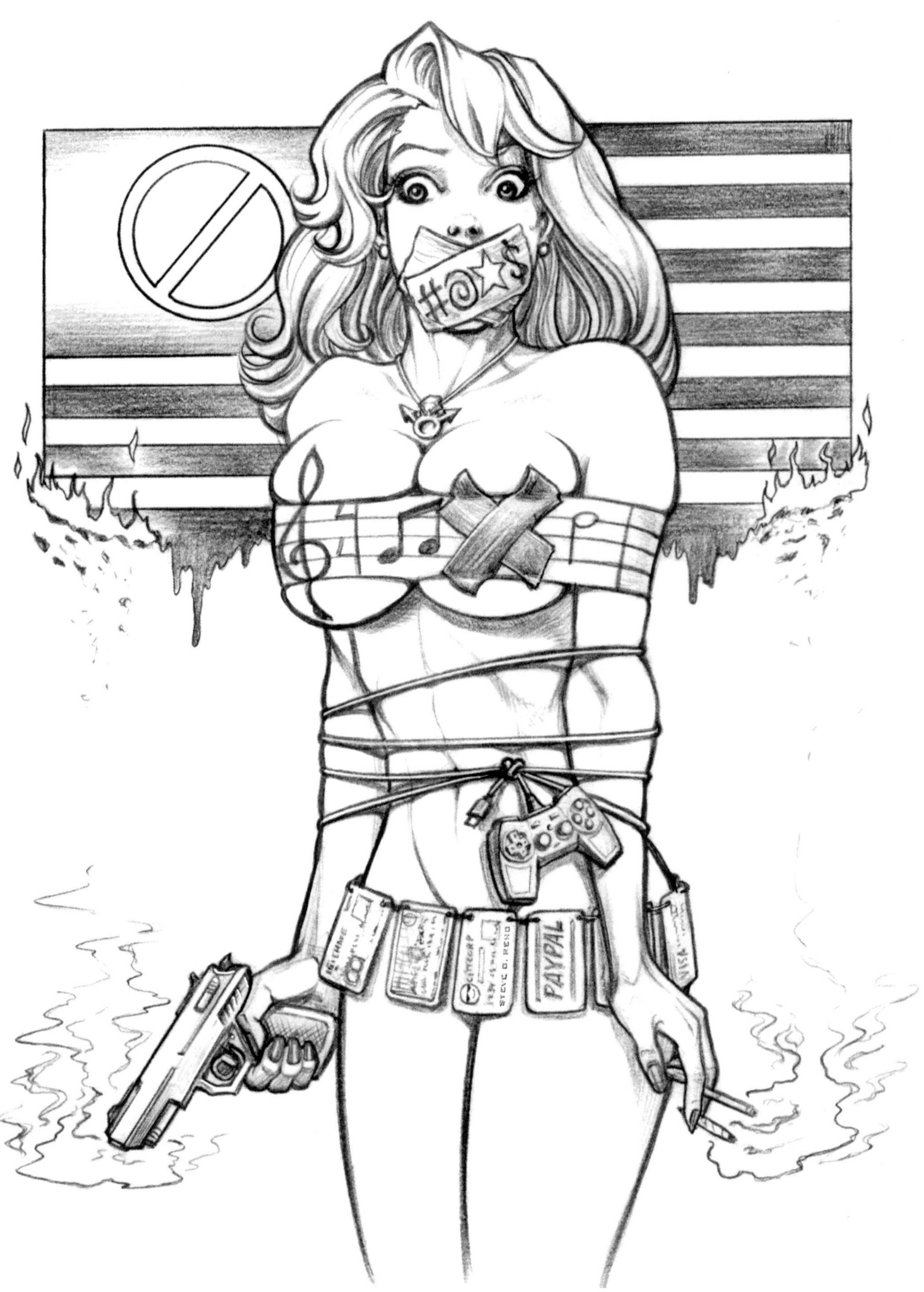

Land of the F...

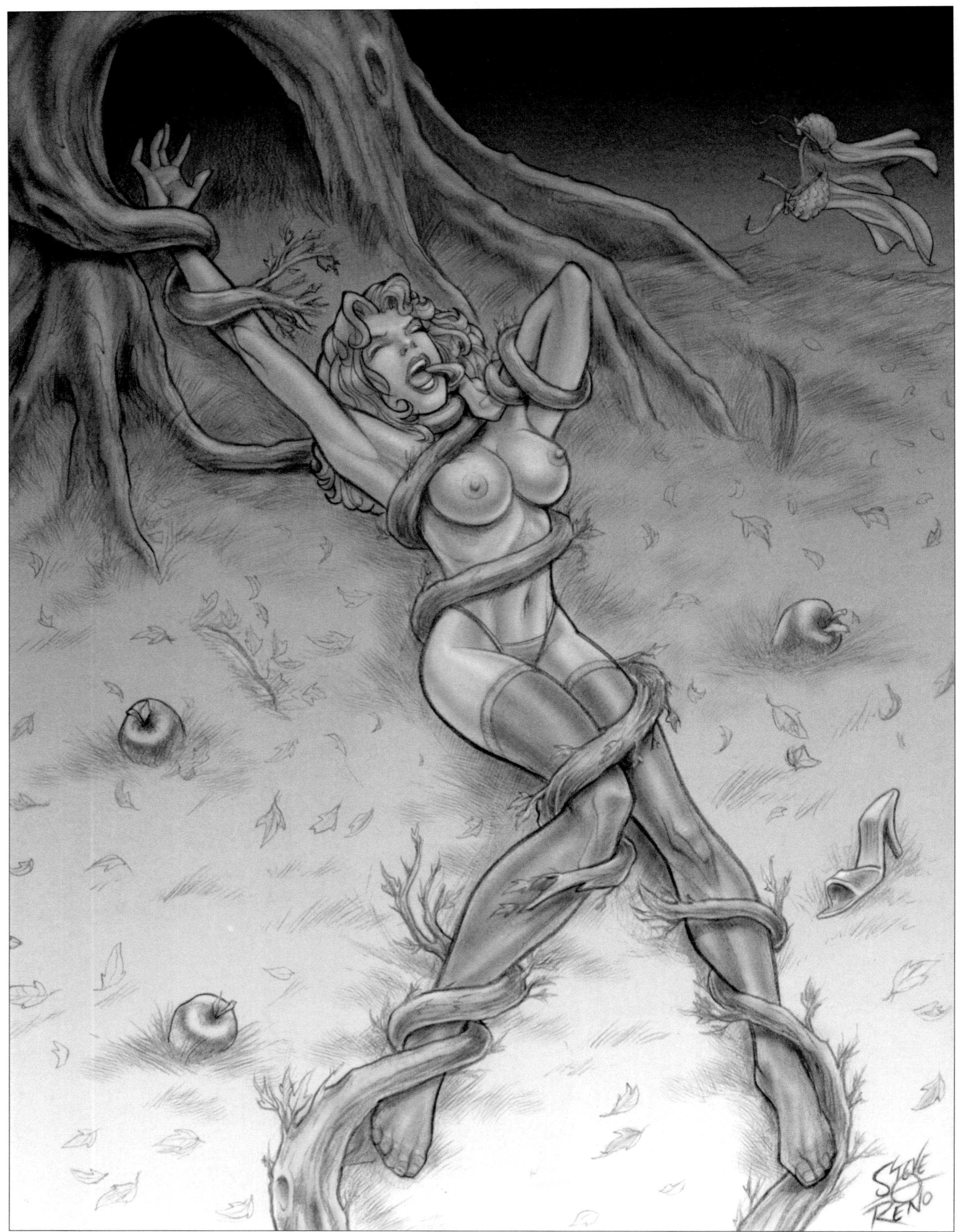

Picking Back